# Solidarity or Barbarism

# Conflict and Consciousness
## Studies in War, Peace, and Social Thought

Charles Webel
*General Editor*

Vol. 3

PETER LANG
New York • Washington, D.C./Baltimore • Boston
Bern • Frankfurt am Main • Berlin • Vienna • Paris

Gianluca Bocchi
and Mauro Ceruti

# Solidarity or Barbarism

## A Europe of Diversity
## Against Ethnic Cleansing

*Translated from the Italian by*
Alfonso Montuori

PETER LANG
New York • Washington, D.C./Baltimore • Boston
Bern • Frankfurt am Main • Berlin • Vienna • Paris

**Library of Congress Cataloging-in-Publication Data**

Bocchi, Gianluca.
[Solidarietà o barbarie. English]
Solidarity or barbarism: a Europe of diversity against ethnic cleansing /
Gianluca Bocchi and Mauro Ceruti; translated by Alfonso Montuori.
p. cm. — (Conflict and consciousness; vol. 3)
Includes bibliographical references.
1. Europe—Politics and government—1989– . 2. Europe—Ethnic relations.
3. Nationalism—Europe. I. Ceruti, Mauro. II. Title. III. Series.
D2009.B6413    940.55—dc21    97-20826
ISBN 0-8204-3147-8
ISSN 1899-9910


**Die Deutsche Bibliothek-CIP-Einheitsaufnahme**

Bocchi, Gianluca:
Solidarity or barbarism: a Europe of diversity against ethnic cleansing /
Gianluca Bocchi and Mauro Ceruti. Transl. by Alfonso Montuori.
–New York; Washington, D.C./Baltimore; Boston; Bern;
Frankfurt am Main; Berlin; Vienna; Paris: Lang.
(Conflict and consciousness; Vol. 3)
ISBN 0-8204-3147-8

Cover design by James F. Brisson.


The paper in this book meets the guidelines for permanence and durability
of the Committee on Production Guidelines for Book Longevity
of the Council of Library Resources.

© 1997 Peter Lang Publishing, Inc., New York

Printed in the United States of America.

# Contents

# Preface

*Edgar Morin*

The historical experiences of the present always cast a different light on the story of the past. The French revolution was therefore reinterpreted during the restoration, during the July Monarchy, during the revolution of 1848, during the Third Republic, during the development of Socialism and then Communism; Post-Stalinism has finally led to the most recent reinterpretation, that of François Furet.

In this book by Gianluca Bocchi and Mauro Ceruti the history of Europe is revisited in the heart of the most recent era, an era of fractures and ruptures, born in 1991, that brutally followed the euphoria after the relaxation of tensions between East and West, the rejection of Stalinism, and the common call of democracy. This story is today retroactively illuminated by the Yugoslavian tragedy, and by the martyrdom of Sarajevo.

In this book, Europe's revisited history is re-articulated and re-constituted in its full complexity. There certainly have been other histories of Europe: but they have all considered international relations and wars far more than the creation and formation of the complex web that is Europe. School texts have, for their part, always conceived of Europe from the perspective of their respective nations. Western texts have typically ignored the East, with exceptions made for the major events tied to Western history, like Lepanto or Sarajevo in 1914. In this book, the resurrection of European complexity naturally represents a polycentric view of European history. The authors' poly-focal *scanning* leads us to see a poly-Europe.

This complex history is seen by Bocchi and Ceruti in its chaotic reality, where chaos is seen as an incessant and tormented dialectic of order, disorder, and organization. In all its chaos, Europe's history has been both creative and destructive. But the originality of this chaos is that it has been continuously generative from the 15th to the 20th century. It has produced a civilization that is constantly in motion, creating among other things secular thought, modern rationality, modern humanism, modern science, modern technology, the nation state, capitalism, and socialism. And another original aspect of this chaos is that, in the end, with the two World Wars, it has been destructive and suicidal. Europe, which developed in chaos, has risked annihilation through that very chaos, and can now only save itself through partnership.

In short, Europe's very creativity has been ambivalent, leading to domination, robbery, conquests, barbarism, and at the same time to the flowers of its philosophy, its poetry, its music, and the ideals of liberty, equality, and fraternity. On the other hand, its very civilization, including science and technology, has created new forms of barbarism.

Revisiting European history was necessary, because we are in an era when we see a return of that which seemed to have been rejected by the ideas of European community, of a universalism that is open to the world, going beyond borders, beyond the absolute sovereignty of the nation state, when religion is limited to guiding private lives rather than the fate of nations.... We are in the era where the dark face of Europe, which had become less visible during the late 70's and seemed to have disappeared in 1989–1990, reappears, tends to become predominant, and indeed becomes mortally threatening.

Bocchi and Ceruti succeed in drawing a history of Europe as polyhistory. They have shown an always renewed dialectic between the forces of homogenization and the forces of diversity, and they have shown how encounters, mixtures, and exchanges are re-creators of diversity. And we should underline the fact that the history of Europe has, in certain moments, been saved from great homogenizations thanks to small islands of great cultural wealth, such as the Tuscan cities of the 15th century, and Amsterdam at the beginning of the 17th century.

On the other hand, Bocchi and Ceruti have shown in a very deep and original way the complexity of notions which are apparently the same, such as nation, state, people, ethnic group (to which one should add the notion of nationality, which is, in turn, not the same as an ethnic group).

Another merit of this book is that it sheds light on how purification is neither a recent accident, nor singularly Serb, nor a purely ethnic phenomenon. Purification is in the logic of dark forces, those which triumphed in Spain in 1492 and in all the forms of religious purification until the revocation of the edict of Nantes by France's Louis XIV. Pushed back by the intermarrying of the great poly-ethnic nations, by the development of toleration, by the de-ghettoization of the Jews, by the opening of the great cosmopolitan capitals, by cultural exchanges of all kinds, the specter of purification returns with nationalism, which at its worst produces the racist illusion.

Finally, this book remembers all the purifications of our century, starting with those provoked by the Greek-Turkish wars with reciprocal exchanges and movements of populations of millions of individuals, then on to the ones provoked by the expulsion or the massacre of Turks in the Balkan states that had been freed from the Ottoman Empire, continuing with the Nazi purifications (of Jews, Gypsies, Poles), Stalin's purifications (mass deportation of ethnic groups considered disloyal), and then at the end of the war of 1939–1945, with the mass deportation of Germans from Silesia, Sudeten, Danzig, Eastern Prussia, and the Balkans, including Yugoslavia.

This in-depth historical look allows us to insist on the solution which, however improbable, is today really vital, namely that of partnership and solidarity. This solution involves a de-dramatization of borders, an awareness of everybody's poly-identity, an awareness of the immense richness of this poly-identity, an awareness of the European reality which is a *unitas multiplex*, and shows us that multiplicity and diversity can be saved only with partnership and solidarity.

This short book, dense, complex, and masterful, should be a manual for students, for teachers, and for citizens.

# 1

## Ethnic cleansing

### Europe against itself

In the history of Europe, ethnic cleansing has not been the exception but the rule.

With ethnic cleansing, Europe has revolted against itself, against its multiple roots.

Bogdan Bogdanovic, former mayor of Belgrade, reminded us in a noble and dramatic warning to his fellow Serbs, and the whole of Europe, that ethnic cleansing cannot produce winners, only losers. In Vukovar and Sarajevo, along with human lives, we have lost the lives of things. In Vukovar and Sarajevo, the aggressors want to eradicate the past. They want to eliminate all traces of history. They want to uproot any sign of pulsing contamination, of solidarities produced by centuries of events, contingencies, ethnic and interpersonal relations....

At the end of one of the most tragic centuries in history, Europe is once again on the threshold of an abyss it has encountered before. It is an abyss in which it has fallen many times.

In our century, as in previous centuries, a Europe that has risked destroying itself by destroying the complexity of its own history has been saved by unexpected allies: nostalgia and memory. Literature, art, architecture, and the territories themselves, are drenched in interactions and mixtures. And for precisely this reason, the purifiers have always been iconoclasts: destroyers of images, books, temples, buildings, territories. Precisely for this reason, all the acts of violence in Europe's history have been accompanied by a repression and a rewriting of memories. But memory is a clever adversary. It is capable of marshaling a thousand resources. It reappears where no one is looking, and is capable of vengeance. The clash between purifiers and diversity has seen the whole of Europe as a battlefield.

Even in our century, in large parts of Europe, and above all in central and Eastern Europe, ethnic cleansing has not been the exception, but the rule.

Ethnic cleansing has been achieved in many different ways.

Throughout our century, migration has been the fate of history's losers. These migrations have often been imposed by fear of the new order, or the desire not to surrender to a new power. For the persecuted ethnicities migrations have been the only way to retain their threatened identity or to recover a lost identity. Often, they have been imposed by the victors themselves, by a newly created state or an occupying foreign power. Sometimes they have been coldly decided at the table of peace treaties, with the conviction—or the pretext—that the "purified" order would be more livable than the earlier orders.

Leaving the homeland behind has been the destiny of a large part of the Islamic populations which had for centuries lived in the Balkans: Turks, and, to a lesser extent, Albanians, Slav Moslems, Pomaks (Islamic Bulgarians). The Ottoman Turks lost three wars in the Balkans, followed by three waves toward Asia: 1878, 1912-1913, 1914-1918.

But the Greeks, even though they were among the great victors in these wars, suffered a similar fate. In turn defeated by the Turks in 1922, they had to abandon in great numbers lands they had lived on in Asia. After the massacres of the wars, Turks and Greeks reached agreement only on the exchange of populations. 400,000 Muslim Turks abandoned the Greek soil they had begun to populate five centuries earlier. The Orthodox Greeks, 1,300,000 of them, abandoned Istanbul, east Thrace, the southern coast of the Black Sea, the Aegean coast of Anatolia, all of which they had begun to populate at least three thousand years earlier, at the time of the founding of Miletus. The logic of these accords (Moslems exchanged for persons of Orthodox faith) created strange situations: Orthodox Arabs found themselves in Greece, Catholic and Protestant Greeks departed from there with great difficulty. The same logic of the accords saved some traces of the past: Greeks stayed in Istanbul, Turks in Greek Western Thrace.

At the end of the second world war, it was the Germans who experienced a nemesis provoked by the Nazi folly. More than 12 million people had to leave the land they had been living on for centuries (Prussia, Pomerania, Silesia, Sudetenland, Banat, Transylvania) and acquired refugee status in the more restricted borders of the new state of West Germany.

After the Second World War, on the other hand, Poland also experienced the drama of a ruined identity reconstituted at the table through Soviet decisions and by the Western acquiescence of what was really a *fait accompli*. With its eastern borders mutilated, separated from lands which had been central to its population and its culture since the Middle Ages, Poland was compensated in the north and west, with large parts of Prussia, Pomerania, and Silesia, regions which since the Middle Ages had been an integral part of the German nation. Five million Poles were involved in this process of uprooting and re-rooting. on a more limited scale, analogous migrations took place in neighboring Czechoslovakia: many colonists from the eastern part of the country (largely Slovaks) settled in the Sudetenland and regions adjacent to the Western border, left practically empty by the German emigration.

The migrations following wars, peace settlements, inter-ethnic conflicts during the years of the great European wars 1914-1945 and its continuation in a cold war have been of even greater dimensions. They involved practically every nationality of central and eastern Europe.

It has been calculated that between 1919 and 1938, the population movements originating in east and central Europe, which remained on European soil (excluding, therefore, frequent migrations to the Americas), affected 21,260,000 individuals: 8 million Germans, 5 million Ukrainians, 3 million Hungarians (Magyars), 1 million Bulgarians, 1 million Byelorussians, 900,000 Russians, 700,000 Albanians, 400,000 Slovenians...

In the period immediately after the Second World War, between 1946 and 1952, the migratory stream involved at least 23,805,000 people: 12,125,000 Germans, 5 million Poles, 3,600,000 among Russians, Ukrainians, Byelorussians, and other nationalities of the Soviet Union, 1,900,000 Slovaks...

Many traditional migratory streams continue to this day. Between 1983 and 1991, a further 1,434,000 persons of German origin returned to Germany from many Eastern and Central European countries (Poland, Soviet Union, Rumania)... To this day, many Russian Jews continue to settle in Israel.

New migratory streams have developed. From East to West, there have been great economic migrations. We find Albanians in Italy, Rumanians in Greece and Turkey, Russians and Rumanians in Poland, Croatians and Hungarians in Austria, all interwoven in a complicated mosaic of survival, which transforms once again the face of these regions.

Starting in 1991, an enormous hemorrhaging of populations also involves the ancient republics of Yugoslavia. Many seek to avoid violence and war through migration. The human landscape risks becoming irrevocably changed: 340,200 persons have sought asylum in Germany, 128,700 in

Hungary, 92,000 in Sweden, 89,700 in Austria, 72,400 in Switzerland, 23,500 in Italy, and 20,300 in Turkey.

At times, external expulsion has been replaced by coerced internal migration. In our century, in the Soviet Union, deportation to lost and distant lands, located in Siberia, the Far East, and central Asia, has been the norm. It has often been prolonged and confused by a partly planned decimation of the peoples involved.

First, during and after the Second World War, Stalin imposed relocation on entire nationalities, from one day to the next, forcing them to travel across vast reaches of his empire. Forced to travel in trucks or wagons intended for oil transport, with no respect for hygiene, with insufficient food, exposed to all kinds of weather, not all of those who were torn from their homelands survived the journey. The number of deaths during the journey was always shocking.

For the survivors, there awaited the dramatic destiny of Siberian deportation camps, or, in the best of cases, the job of cultivating the virgin soil of the steppes of central Asia, thousands of miles from their places of origin.

The Ukrainians were the first victims of large scale ethnic deportation, often confused and interlinked with political deportation, of which Russians themselves were victims. The Ukrainian ruling class and intelligentsia were decimated with the ritual charge of "bourgeois nationalism."

After September of 1939, when the infamous pact between Hitler and Stalin gave the Soviet Union control over the northern section of Poland, at least a million people were forcibly removed from this region (Poles, Jews, Ukrainians, Byelorussians...). In those same years, some 14,000 of the best and brightest Polish Army officers and soldiers were killed.

Immediately afterwards, the same fate struck the inhabitants of the Baltic countries, when in the summer of 1940, the Soviet Union forcibly annexed Latvia, Estonia, and Lithuania. The next year, in 1941, there was a new wave of deportations. Stalin feared that the approaching German troops would somehow benefit from the anti-Russian feeling in that region. Only 20% of the Baltic deportees managed to return to their lands after the war.

Many Germans had lived on Russian soil, particularly in Ukraine and on the lower course of the Volga, since the eighteenth century. Between the two wars the Soviet regime had given them an autonomous republic (the region of Saratov) and 17 national districts. In August of 1941, Stalin accused them of collusion with the enemy. He suppressed their autonomous republic, and sent them *en masse* to Siberia, Kazakhstan, and Kirgyztan. The same fate struck the Koreans who lived in a completely different area, the far east on the coast of the Pacific. The reason: their motherland, Korea, had been annexed by the Japanese empire, and was now enemy territory.

The list of "punished peoples" was growing. Stalin's suspicions focused on many small peoples living in the Caucasus region of the Black Sea. He accused them of treachery during the war, even though in some cases the Germans had not even come near their territories. Between 1943 and 1947, Kalmuks, Kara-Kalpaks, Balkars, Chechens, Ingush, Crimean Tartars, Meskets, became part of this fearsome list. Their autonomous territories were suppressed, and around 2 million people had to confront a difficult exile.

All these peoples were swallowed up by obscurity until 1956, when Khruschev, at the Twentieth Congress, and began the post-Stalinist thaw.

At the end of the year, a decree rehabilitated Kalmucks, Kara-Kalpaks, Balkars, Chechens, and Ingush peoples. Between 1957 and 1959, they were able to return to their lands and once again obtain the administrative autonomy they enjoyed before the war. The Kara-Kalpaks and Balkars found their valleys empty: no one had occupied them. Not so for the Ingush: one part of their territory had been given to neighboring Ossetians. Thus started a fierce rancor that, in the early nineties, developed into one of the many open conflicts in the tormented post-Soviet Caucasus.

For less lucky peoples, the Siberian and Asian exile continued. They were not heard from again until the Eighties, during the time of Gorbachev and *Perestroika*, when they could make their voices count with the help of public opinion both national and international.

Today, the destiny of these peoples is still uncertain.

The Germans had, and still have, the good luck of being supported by a rich and authoritative nation-state. In recent years they have largely returned to the lands of their ancestors, Germany. The communities that have been left behind are asking for the restoration of the German republic in the region of the Volga, along with a new autonomous territory in Eastern Prussia around Kaliningrad (Königsberg), which was part of German territory and inhabited by Germans until 1945. The Crimean Tartars had to help themselves, but in the years of Perestroika their voice has been heard loud and clear. They have started to trickle back to their land of origin and then, gradually, the flux intensified. Today, of about 400,000 people, more than half have returned to Crimea, where they have to face the hostility of the Russians and Ukrainians who have taken possession of their lands.

Moreover, a delicate conflict has developed: the Russian majority is ready to ask for secession from Ukraine and the return to Russia, to which she belonged until 1954.

Finally, the Meskets (Moslem and Turkish Georgians) have not only not been rehabilitated, but have almost all stayed in Uzbekistan, the place of their deportation. Here they have become scapegoats, victims of ethnic uprisings by the local populations. It is only recently that some have managed to return, one by one, to the Caucasus.

And there is finally the extreme manifestation of ethnic cleansing: the physical elimination of entire collectivities, for ethnic or religious reasons, including genocide, and the annihilation of a sizable part of an entire ethnic group.

At the turn of the century, ethnic massacres took place during all the wars and the periods of armed peace in the Balkans. From 1898 to 1902, Macedonian terrorists made more than 4,000 Turkish victims. The Turkish repression in 1903 caused an equal number of victims, this time Macedonian.

When the First World War broke out, many ethnic minorities were hit very hard, suspected of possible deals with the enemy. In every territory, many individuals were imprisoned or killed under the flimsiest pretexts.

The principal ethnic victims of the war were those belonging to a group seeking national independence: the Armenians. For thousands of years, the principal nucleus of their population was located in the lands of Eastern Anatolia and the Southern Caucasus. In 1914, a large number of Armenians lived in the Ottoman Empire. When the war broke out, they began to act as fifth columnists for the enemies of the Ottoman Empire: the Russians and the English. In this way, they hoped to bring the moment of liberation nearer.

The historic home of the Armenians, Eastern Anatolia, was close to the Russian border. The Armenians played an important role in expediting the advance of the Czarist troops. The Ottoman empire reacted by decreeing mass deportation. The Armenians were forced to move hundreds of kilometers South, to Syria.

At least a million Armenians were affected. Only 30,000 survived the war and the deportation. Many were massacred along the road, in clashes with local Turkish or Kurdish communities. Many were killed for purely economic motives, to be deprived of the few possessions they had brought with them. Many others died because of the journey itself, because of cold, heat, hunger, exhaustion, illnesses.

The Armenians did not return to the lands they had to abandon. They survived scattered in many places: Istanbul, France, the United States, Syria itself. The Armenians who remained in the Russian Caucasus were integrated in the new Soviet Union, and took part in its affairs.

Having become even harder and more aggressive between the two wars, nationalism passed another threshold of barbarism. The desire for absolute victory over the enemy, over ethnicities and states labeled as enemies, pushed not only for the denial of the right of the conquered peoples to self-government, but to dismember its community of states, and to prohibit the use of its language, and to annihilate its culture. And, with clear mind and aberrant rhetoric, the very right of physical survival was being denied.

In 1941, Ante Pavélic, dictator of the puppet state of Croatia enslaved by the Nazis, declared absolute war on all individuals and collectivities considered "not nationals" in his state: Serbs, Jews, and gypsies. His massacres were the sinister accompaniment of the cruelty in which the whole of central and eastern Europe had degenerated under the heel of Hitler's armies.

When Hitler invaded Bohemia, in March of 1939, he ordered that half the Czechs be "eliminated," and the rest serve as a work force. When he invaded Poland, in September of the same year, he ordered the massacre of all the nobility and clergy. In 1942, when Ukraine and Russia also looked on the brink of Nazi enslavement, the following concept reappeared: the conquered peoples were to work for their new masters; they were not to receive more food than absolutely necessary; those who did not serve might as well die.... All accompanied by delirious assertions about racial destinies and the biological predestination of nations.

Fortunately, there was not much time for the massacres to reach their extreme consequences. In the span of two years, the tides of the war changed, and the Nazis abandoned the Slavic regions. But the Second World War made a profound mark of the demographics of the whole of Central and Eastern Europe. 22 million people had died.

In this horrendous journey, the Holocaust is an even more distant threshold: perhaps the last and supreme threshold. For Jews and Gypsies, the final solutions was not "fifty/fifty." Jews and Gypsies were simply to have been eliminated.

In vast regions of central and eastern Europe, the disgraceful Nazi plan was largely completed. The Nazis annihilated 92% of Polish Jews, 89% of

Latvian Jews, 87% of Lithuanian Jews, 80% of Greek Jews, 75% of Hungarian Jews, 73% of Yugoslavian Jews, 75% of Czechoslovakian Jews, 47% of Rumanian Jews, 43% of Soviet Jews, 81% of Austrian Jews, 78% of German Jews, 75% of Dutch Jews. To the great number of Jewish victims we must add also a great number of gypsies (205,000 in the Central and Eastern European countries alone).

The space that had been created was increased in the years after the war by emigration to Israel by a large contingent of the Jews who had remained on European soil. This emigration continued and is continuing to this day, following a multiplicity of hostilities: that of the Soviet regime as well as present-day Russian ultra-nationalists.

The Terror and the Holocaust, final thresholds of barbarism of the closure of European minds, have left a crude and lengthy imprint on the life of the continent. The landscape of humanity, the architecture, the social, linguistic, ethnic, cultural, spiritual landscape of ancient regions have been normalized, simplified, impoverished, denatured. Salonika and Vilnius: our century has dealt heavy blows to the Jerusalem of the Baltic and the Jerusalem of the North, symbol-cities in which the various monotheistic faiths of Europe's recent history lived side by side, in a difficult but nevertheless possible relationship. More than 60,000 Jews lived in Soloun/Selanik/Thessalonika at the beginning of the century, the Jerusalem of the Balkans, where synagogues, mosques, and Orthodox cathedrals, were interwoven in the urban fabric. Today, approximately 1,300 Jews remain, carefully conserving two synagogues and a small museum, memories of the past.

Between Greece, Serbia, and Bulgaria is a region of uncertain ownership, with a name that has become proverbial in many European languages: Macedonia. Ethnicities and religions were all mixed together: cities were known by double, triple, quadruple names. Turkish, the imperial language, resonated with the Slavic languages (Bulgarian, Serbian, and a series of intermediate dialects, which linguists came to call Macedonian); with the Greek language of the ancient Byzantine empire; with Wallachian, (Armenian), which still carried the remote traces of Rome's dominion; with Albanian, descended from an even more distant wave of population; with archaic Spanish (*ladino*) which had been brought by Sephardic Jews expelled from the Iberian peninsula centuries earlier.

In the first fifty years of our century, this land saw a war in which many Christian nations created a coalition to divide among themselves the remains of the Ottoman empire; a new war in which the Christian nations contested among each other those remains; the igniting of the first world war; the cavalry of the Serbian army, which crossed the hostile Albanian mountains in winter; a new war between Greeks and Turks; the exchange of populations between Greeks and Turks; the war between Italians and Greeks; the dismemberment of Yugoslavia; the occupation of Greece; the Nazi massacres; the Holocaust; the partisan war of liberation; the new Soviet empire; the Stalinist Terror; the Greek civil war; Tito's schism....

In the Thirties, more than 60,000 Jews lived in Vilnius, the Jerusalem of the North, where synagogues, Orthodox cathedrals, Catholic churches, along with Tartar mosques, were woven into the Urban fabric. Today, there are barely 1,500 left, carefully trying to restore the only synagogue which escaped devastation.

Between Poland, Lithuania, Byelorussia, and Ukraine, there was the region of uncertain ownership which the Jews called *Lita* and the Poles *Kresy* ("borders"). The ethnicities and religions were all mixed together; the cities had double, triple, quadruple names. Lithuanian, language of a people which narrated ancient Indo-European myths and still carried the traces of a more remote Pre-Indo-European world, resonated with the Byelorussian of the countryside; with Polish prevalent in literature and administration; with the languages of the Germans and Russians, colonizers from distant lands; with Yiddish, German in structure and of partly Hebrew vocabulary, brought by the Ashkenazi Jews that had escaped the persecutions by Western Christianity.

In the first fifty years of our century, this land witnessed the Czarist anti-semitism; the bloody clash between the German and Russian empires; the peace between the Kaiser and the Bolshevik revolutionaries; the war between the new Soviet power and a resurgent Poland; a clash between Poland and Lithuania about borders and territorial possessions; a clash between Germany and Lithuania about borders and territorial possessions; the nationalist hardening of Poles and Lithuanians; the suppression of Byelorussian schools and magazines by both Russians and Poles; the Nazi ultimatum to the Lithuanians; the Nazi ultimatum to the Poles; the temporary and horrific alliance between Nazism and Stalinism; the Stalinist ultimatum to the Poles; the first Stalinist Terror; the Nazi invasion and ensuing massacres; the Holocaust; the second Stalinist terror; Soviet anti-semitism; the internal and external empires of the Soviet union.

At the beginning of the Twentieth century, many Jews, both Sephardic and Ashkenazi, lived in Sarajevo, capital of Bosnia-Herzegovina, brought to this ethnic crucible by the events of many centuries. During the Second World War they were hit very hard by the massacres of Ante Pavélic, or at least forced to emigrate. But for all the events of this century, the two Balkan wars, the two World Wars, Nazism and Stalinism, until 1992 one centuries-old community of three peoples speaking the same language had survived. They did not feel part of the same ethnicity: different and divergent stories had created distinct identities for Catholics (Croatians), Orthodox (Serbs), and Moslems.

# 2

## Bosnia and Europe

### A recurring story

Since antiquity, the regions of what today is Bosnia-Herzegovina have been lands of contacts, encounters, and clashes. In the days of the Roman Empire, they were populated by numerous Illyrian tribes, an ancient Indo-European people that had lived in the Balkans for centuries. It was these peoples who were subjected to the influx of Latin civilization from the West, and Greek civilization from the East. In the first centuries of the Middle Ages, many northern Slavic tribes settled there. They dominated the ancient ethnicities, but not completely. For centuries they coexisted with the Latin and Greek branches. At the beginning of the modern age, in surrounding regions we would find Wallachians and Dalmatians, two neo-Latin peoples, along with Albanians, who are most likely, descendants of the Illyrians.

The encounters/clashes between Greek and Latin civilizations in the classical age were followed in the Middle Ages by encounters/clashes between Latin and Byzantine Christianity. Bordering Slavic tribes became Catholic or Orthodox, depending on their exposure to Roman or Byzantine doctrined. Islamic influences arrived later, after 1400, when the Ottoman Turks suppressed the ancient Slavic states of the Balkans. Generally, Balkan Slavs lost their political independence, but not their religious identity. They remained either Orthodox or Catholic.

But Bosnia was a special case: in this region a large number of the Bosnian Slavs converted to the Moslem religion.

In the Middle Ages, the Bogomilan heresy spread in Bosnia, and its followers were persecuted by the surrounding Christians. In the eyes of the persecuted, therefore, the Turks appeared as liberators. In any case, for the Ottomans, Bosnia always remained a border land, standing against their adversaries: the Habsburg Empire and the Republic of Venice. Perhaps more was asked of border populations, greater loyalty and greater integration including their faith.

At the end of the seventeenth century, almost all the areas populated by Orthodox Serbs and Catholic Croats were under Ottoman control. In the eighteenth century, the Habsburg Empire regained a good part of the ancient reign of Croatia: for more than a century, the Croatian people were divided by the border of two empires. At the beginning of the nineteenth century, Serbia begin to separate itself from Ottoman domination. It became an autonomous principality, then an independent state. But the regions of Bosnia, even those which contained strong Serb centers, remained in Turkish possession. A frontier also divided the Serb people, and for the Serbs, Bosnia became unredeemed land.

In 1878, the decisions and accords of the great European powers assigned all of Bosnia-Herzegovina to the Austro-Hungarian Empire, as the Austrian Empire had recently come to be known. To the frontier dividing Serbs, a new frontier was added, separating the Bosnian Moslem Slavs from the Turks, their protectors and co-religionists, with whom they felt ethnically united.

The Croatians, on the other hand, were united in a single empire. But their unity was illusory. The nucleus of Croatia belonged to the Hungarian half of the empire, which after 1867 became a state in its own right. The Dalmatian coastline, rich in Croatian centers, remained under Austria. For its part, Bosnia-Herzegovina became an imperial possession of peculiarly uncertain status. Until 1908, it was mandated to Austria-Hungary by the other powers. After 1908, it was annexed by the empire, but was administered directly from the center, without becoming part of either half: it became a dependency of the ministry of finance, one of the few institutions held in common by Austria and Hungary. The Croatian people—aspiring to unity and self-government—had, in fact, been divided in three.

In 1910, Bosnia-Herzegovina counted 43.5% Orthodox Serbs, 32.2% Moslems, and 22.9% Catholics Croatians. None of the three peoples was satisfied. The Habsburg government created and destroyed a web of compromises and concessions: *divide et impera*.

The claims of the Bosnian peoples were becoming part of a larger plot.

In those years, all of the territories of the multi-national empire were the subject of lively dispute. Would the need for autonomy and self-government, coming from all corners and nationalities of the empire, result in the destruction of the empire? Or would the Habsburg monarchy be able to survive, through reform and the ability to balance these nationalist claims? A first indication in this latter direction was what in 1867 had been defined as

*Ausgleich*, or "compromise." The empire was divided into two bodies, separate but united by the crown and other constraints: Austria (*Cisleithania*) and Hungary (*Transleithania*). The Hungarian claims had largely been defused and satisfied. On the other hand, the claims of Croatians and Transylvanian Rumanians, who from then felt oppressed by the Hungarians were exacerbated.

The number of Slavic people in the empire was much greater than either Germans or Hungarians. Would a "compromise" also be possible with them? Would a triple monarchy be created?

There were some obvious difficulties. In the empire, western Slavs (Czechs, Slovaks, Poles) and eastern Slavs (Ukrainians) were separated from the southern Slavs (Slovenians, Croatians, Serbs) by land densely populated with Hungarians and Germans. Also, many Slavs were governed by Austria, from Vienna; many others by Hungary, from Budapest; and yet others constituted the "separate body" of Bosnia-Herzegovina.

Faced with the web of ethnicities and the multiplicity of national claims, more innovative solutions seemed conceivable. The Austrian socialists ("Austro-Marxists") proposed a reform of imperial territories, to be divided into federal units of medium size with ample powers. The new federal units (*gubernia*) were not conceived along purely ethnic or geographic lines. They were to be regional entities whose identities were defined, case by case, by the interweaving of ethnic, geographic, historical, and economic identities. For the reorganization of the Austrian half of the empire, Karl Renner had proposed 8 federal units:

| | |
|---|---|
| 1. Galicia-Bukovina | (majority: Polish; principal minorities: Ukrainian, Rumanian, German) |
| 2. Bohemia | (majority: Czech; principal minority: German) |
| 3. Moravia-Silesia | (majority: Czech; principal minorities: German, Polish) |
| 4. Carniola-Littoral | (majority: Slovenians; principal minorities: Italian, Croatian, German) |
| 5. Lower Austria | (majority: German) |
| 6. Upper Austria | (majority: German) |
| 7. Tyrol-Vorarlberg | (majority: German; principal minorities: Italian) |
| 8. Styria-Carinthia | (majority: German principal minorities: Slovenians) |

In 1914, two national projects divided the allegiances of the Slavs of Bosnia-Herzegovina. The first aimed at unity and self-government for the southern Slavs (Serbs, Croatians, Slovenians, Bosnian Moslems) who were part of the empire, and compatible with reform: in 1905, the Fiume Resolutions had proposed the transformation of the double monarchy into a triune kingdom. The second project looked outward. The unity of the southern Slavs would be made possible by their secession from the empire, by the extension of a more homogeneous Slavic nucleus: the Serbian nation-state, which had gained new territories in the two Balkan wars (1912–1913).

The plotters who, on the 28 of June 1914, assassinated archduke Francis Ferdinand, heir to the Habsburg throne, were followers of a pan-Slavic ideology. It has been said that the shots fired by Gavrilo Princip caused more than 8 million deaths, the result of World War I, which broke out a month later through events set in motion by the assassination. The assassination, in Sarajevo, was a small cause which quickly provoked a large effect: a great historical wave that enveloped all Europe.

In the summer of 1914, when the Austro-Hungarian troops marched against Serbia, when the European powers trapped themselves in a game of reciprocal ultimatums and mobilizations, none of the parties involved knew it was on the brink of unleashing a great European war, which would last at least thirty years. In fact, general opinion was that the war would be short and circumscribed. It was difficult to perceive that the tried and true European "Balance of Power" system was breaking down. But the new idea of national citizenship and the system of rights and duties which this idea involved had ensured a general citizens' mobilization. The era of professional armies was over. Everybody was now unavoidably involved in the conflict.

The conflict drifted out of control. Two subtle and sensitive historians, Krzystof Pomian and François Fejtoe, have pointed out that, during World War I, a transformation occurred in the way the imagination of the European people conceived of the very idea of conflict, with devastating consequences. War became total, rather than limited. It became ideological. War was not fought to turn the enemy away, to trap the enemy or obtain concessions. From now on the enemy was to be annihilated. Victory was no longer to be determined by a particular goal. It seemed imposed by the rationality of history itself. Of course, this rationality was claimed by each of the players. The enemy had to be annihilated because he was deemed backward from the perspective of inevitable progress.

Along with this rhetoric, during the war years, the idea began to appear that the era of great multi-national empires (such as the Austro-Hungarian Empire and the Ottoman Empire) was over, and that it would be possible and desirable to extend throughout the whole European continent the model of the nation-state, the form of political organization characteristic of Western Europe in the past few centuries. At that point a subtle game began to develop among the future victors of the conflict—France, Great Britain, the United States—and the various national elites of many of the peoples in the Habsburg Empire, who would have benefited from its disintegration. The conference held by these elites in Rome in 1918 was decisive: a centuries old player in the games of European equilibrium, Austria-Hungary would be divided and dismembered. To this day, there is still debate over whether this division was really desired by those living in the empire.

In order to realize the objectives of the victors, a form of geopolitical surgery would be necessary, presenting enormous problems: a clear delimitation of the German and Slav presence in central and eastern Europe; the separation of the multiple nationalities of the dissolved empire; the broadening and consolidation of the Balkan nation-states (these embryonic states, born at the expense of the Ottoman Empire during the nineteenth century, had demonstrated their weakness and engaged in continuous border scuffles). New and numerous borders would have to be traced.

This geopolitical surgery was begun, after the collapse of the central empires at the end of 1918, by the victorious powers (France, Great Britain, the United States) and their allies (Italy, Serbia, Rumania, Greece). In 1919 and 1920, some treaties were negotiated with the defeated countries that were supposed to establish a long lasting European order: the Treaty of Versailles (with Germany, which had turned from an empire into a republic); the Treaty of Saint-Germain-en-Laye (with Austria, considered to be the heir of the Western half of the Habsburg Empire); the Treaty of Neuilly (with Bulgaria); the Treaty of the Trianon (with Hungary, considered to be the heir of the eastern half of the Habsburg Empire); the Treaty of Sèvres (with the Ottoman Empire, which shortly became Turkey).

The major defect in the way these treaties were conceived was the confusion, by no means explicit, between two divergent and often incompatible criteria.

The first criterion, openly declared, objective and desirable, was the principle of nationality. The example of the last century would be followed: the Italians and the Germans had concluded their projects to build nation-states; with the retreat of the Ottoman Empire, new states had also emerged in the Balkans around local ethnicities (Greece, Serbia, Montenegro, Rumania, Albania, Bulgaria). It was now to be hoped that the ethnicities which populated Austria-Hungary (Poles, Czechs, Slovaks, Croatians, Slovenians) would have an analogous form of self-government.

But in areas with populations that had always been mixed, it was impossible to trace a border that did not provoke conflict and resentment. At that point a new criterion intervened, but this time covertly: the states, old and new, were rigorously divided between winners and losers. The winners included Italy, Rumania, Greece (who had fought with the Allies) and the new states of Yugoslavia, Czechoslovakia, and Poland. The losers included Germany, Austria, Hungary, Bulgaria, and Turkey. In an overwhelming number of cases, contested and undecidable on an ethnic basis, the winners were rewarded and losers were penalized.

Rumania, allied with the West, not only annexed Transylvania, (a Habsburg area containing a Rumanian majority), it was also rewarded with territories with Hungarian majorities, and multi-national populations (Banat, Bukovina), in order to define a strategically favorable Western border. Similarly, Italy received the areas of Trento and Trieste and the Istrian coast, (with an Italian ethnic majority), Bolzano and Tarvisio (with a German majority), and regions with Slovenian and Croatian majorities, precisely so it would extend to the border of the Alps, considered "natural" and militarily advantageous.

Opposite criteria were applied to the Germans and the Hungarians. The borders between Germany and Poland, Germany and Czechoslovakia, Austria and Czechoslovakia, were established giving the new states a good part of the areas with mixed populations and even German majorities (the Sudetenland). The fate of the Hungarians was perhaps even worse. The new Hungarian nation-state was very restricted, and left a considerable portion of Magyarophones outside its borders (Czechoslovakia, Rumania, Yugoslavia).

Even more problematic was the creation of states that were constituted by a mosaic of ethnicity (with no definite majority), whose rules of coexistence were far from clear.

Yugoslavia is emblematic. The idea of a free association of Slavic peoples who had lived in the Austro-Hungarian Empire and the Balkan states (Serbia and Montenegro) that had emerged with the retreat of the Ottoman Empire, had found support amongst all these peoples: Croats, Slovenians, Serbs, Montenegrins. But there was another idea, contrary to the idea of an association of Slavs, which placed the Serbs amongst the victors and the Croatians amongst the vanquished. This second idea left traces in the politics of the western powers, and was tempting to Serbian politicians and parties. From the beginning, therefore, Yugoslavia was conceived as a centralized state, leaving little or almost no autonomy to the individual states. In a less dramatic way, conflicts of the same kind marked the origins of the multi-national state of Czechoslovakia: the Slovaks felt subordinate to the Czechs, and other ethnicities (Germans, Hungarians, Poles, Ukrainians) looked sentimentally towards the homelands from which they had been separated.

The treaties were ignored the very minute they were signed. From 1918 to 1924, all of Central and Eastern Europe was shaken by a series of conflicts which were resolved partly with pure force, partly by taking into consideration the inhabitants of the territories in question, partly with more or less subtle compromises which at times were simply left hanging. Italy and Yugoslavia clashed over Fiume; Austria and Yugoslavia over the region bordering Styria and Carinthia; Poland and Czechoslovakia argued over the city and region of Cieszyn/Teschen; Poland and Lithuania argued over Vilnius; Lithuania and Germany over the city and region of Memel; Germany and Poland over Danzig, High Silesia, a part of Eastern Prussia; and so on. At times, the parties openly declared war, as was the case between Germany and Turkey. Other times, new treaties were needed, like the Treaty of Lausanne, which ended the war between Greeks and Turks, partly canceling the arrangements made at Sèvres, or like the Treaty of Rapallo, which fixed the borders between Italy and Yugoslavia.

The collapse of the Czarist empire, the war between revolutionaries and counter-revolutionaries throughout Russia, chaos on the borders of the ancient empires (between Russia and Germany, Russia and Austria-Hungary, and Russia and the Ottoman Empire), all occurring around the same time, did nothing but add to the conflicts.

After the October Revolution of 1917, the Communists controlled only a fraction of the Czarist empire. The Bolsheviks were subjected to attacks and enemies of all kinds. The supporters of the old order were numerous, armed, and present in many regions. Warlords were springing up everywhere, ready to plunder this or that area and make alliances purely for convenience. Any regions that were close to foreign borders, like the Ukraine and the Caucasus had either proclaimed independence or were about to. On the borders, for thousands of kilometers, were foreign enemies: Germany, Austria-Hungary and the Ottoman Empire. Meanwhile, previous allies—France and Germany—had revealed themselves hostile to the new regime, and not for fear of ideological contagion in Europe. They, above all, feared for their new conquests in the Middle East. Great Britain, moreover, saw a threat to its sphere of influence from the Bosphorus all the way to India, which it hoped to build with the spoils of war.

Too many enemies all at once. In order to confront the internal enemies, the Bolshevik regime decided first of all to end external conflicts. In early 1918, the regime negotiated—at Brest-Litovsk—a series of treaties with Germany, the Austro-Hungarian Empire, and the Ottoman Empire, leaving old enemies with a free hand in the Baltic, in Western Ukraine, and in many areas of the Caucasus. The retreat proved timely and providential. In the space of a few years, from 1918 to 1922, the new power managed to end the process of internal fragmentation, and took to the offensive. It did not just regain the continuity and unity of the Russian population's territory, but reached foreign borders very close to those of the Czarist Empire. The Soviet Union was born on December 30, 1922, when the new power returned to old positions in Central Asia and the Caucasus. It had regained Ukraine, which was included in the four founding republics. It had fought another bloody war against the new Polish state, which ended inconclusively: the Soviet power kept the eastern part of Byelorussia, where it installed another republic.

Only in 1924 could World War I really be said to be over in all these regions. In Central and Eastern Europe alone, it left behind more than 3 million war dead. Many more Russians died in that same period, because of civil war, famine, and disease.

The Central and Eastern European states had an extremely varied ethnic composition and yet, at the same time, they were built around the identity of a single ethnic majority which wanted to create a new national imagination, in which it would take a privileged position. This applied not just to Yugoslavia and Czechoslovakia, which ran the same risks of fragmentation as the previous empires. It also applied to Rumania and Poland, homelands of consistent and diversified ethnic minorities. For Hungary, on the other hand, the problem was exactly the other way around: internally relatively homogeneous, it was concerned about individuals of Hungarian culture and language in neighboring states.

The weakest point of the new order was that almost all the peoples and ethnicities of Central and Eastern Europe felt damaged. They were waiting for reparations, in the form of a more or less violent change in borders and power relations. The peoples who had been considered vanquished in peace treaties (Germans, Hungarians, Bulgarians) were now joined by those who felt oppressed in the new multi-national states. On the other hand, even the victors had complaints: for many Yugoslavians, the border with Italy was not at all satisfactory, nor was the border with Czechoslovakia satisfactory for many Poles.

After only fourteen years, in which every majority ethnicity exercised internal cultural oppression and expressed claims against those outside its national borders, the situation came to a head. An aggressive and delirious nationalism, Nazism, appropriated the idea of total victory, and kept pushing this idea further, beyond any limit. It added to these claims of an ethnic basis, shared initially by many Germans, a claim of a completely different and terrifying order: the request for *lebensraum*, or living space, and the need to annex regions never previously inhabited by Germans on the basis of ravings about the so-called vitality of peoples. Out of control, the ideas of ideological war and total victory generated the worst monsters, and disguised a tragic reality made of oppression and exploitation.

From 1938 to 1941, the old order collapsed like a house of cards, also because the Nazis wanted to appear condescending towards the claims of other nations and other peoples who felt damaged by the old order. In 1938–39, the Nazis dismembered Czechoslovakia, with the assent and involvement of Hungarians and Poles; in 1939, they dismembered Poland, thanks to an accord with the Soviets; in 1941, they dismembered Yugoslavia, with the collaboration of Italians, Bulgarians, and Hungarians. The divisions suggested by the Nazis always found interested allies. With the alliance of the Nazis, Hungary and Bulgaria could enlarge their nation-states. With the alliance of the Nazis, Slovaks and Croatians planned simulated states, under the dictatorship of the most reactionary fascists and the most hysterical nationalists.

The Soviet Union was also part of the group of nations dissatisfied with the post-war order. Soviet foreign policy, conducted under the banner of unlimited expansion, began to look more and more like Czarist autocracy and Great-Russia chauvinism. At the first occasion, created by the weakness and lack of unity of neighboring states, Hitler's aggression, and the indecisiveness of the Western powers, Stalin started to remodel his new states along the lines of the old Czarist Empire. In 1939–40, the annexation of Eastern Poland, Rumanian Bessarabia (which became the Republic of Moldavia), Estonia, Latvia, and Lithuania, brought the Soviet borders very close to what they had been up to 1914. If some regions, like Finland, were left out, others were included that had never been part of the Czar's territory: Polish Galicia, and Rumanian Bukovina, for centuries part of the Habsburg Empire.

The order forced upon Europe by Nazi violence was shattered in a few years, leaving behind it an enormous number of casualties. In 1945, the Soviet Union burst into this vacuum, with no possibility of resistance: Nazi oppression had either decimated or forced the emigration of previous ruling elites, the armies, and the cultural élites of states wiped from the face of the map, or forced into an alliance with the Axis. The Soviet Union swiftly filled the void, pushing its territory, and above all its sphere of influence, as far west as possible.

The Soviet Union's victory seemed to have ended a conflict whose roots went deep into a confrontation of civilizations that had been a constant in the last millennium of European history: the confrontation between Slavs and Germans. Since the High Middle Ages, the two ethnic branches had coexisted, interacted, fought, and had—in turn—chased each other and been subjected to each other in the very heart of the European continent. In the modern age, the Russian Empire on the one hand and the Habsburg Empire and Kingdom of Prussia on the other, had repeatedly entered into conflict. From the eighteenth century, the Eastern coast of the Baltic, Poland, the Balkans themselves, became areas of fracture between two movements going in opposite directions. It was precisely the very large number of potential conflicts that led the great powers to a policy of partition of the intermediate territories, at the expense of the smaller peoples there. In 1939, the accord between Hitler and Stalin seemed to place the two totalitarian regimes in the tradition of the empires that had preceded them. Two years later, it became clear that the obsession with total victory at any cost had provoked a kind of inebriation in Nazism. Hitler wanted to see scorched earth in the plains of Russia and the Ukraine, and instead found the seeds of his own destruction.

The end of the Second World War threw Europe into an unexpected situation, in many ways one without precedents. Above all, Europe was out of balance. No single power in the Modern Age had controlled such vast territories as those which came to be part of the Soviet sphere of influence. Moreover, no European country was self-sufficient anymore in matters of defense. The appeal to the American umbrella, the search for a new center external to the continent, was a historical discontinuity which many interpreted as the inevitable decline of Europe.

The most obvious aspect of the new European order was the division of central Europe—which had always been the heart of the continent—into two parts divided by economies, political regimes, and worldviews: two parts which seemed destined to become ever more distant. Linguistic use seemed, at the same time, the most probing sign in the consolidation of this new reality. The terms habitually used before 1945—Central Europe, *Mitteleuropa*—almost disappeared from use. They were replaced by a drastic partition between Western Europe (from the Atlantic to Hamburg, from Lisbon to Trieste) and Eastern Europe (from Stettin to the Black Sea, from Prague to the Urals).

After 1945, the new Soviet empire became a two-tiered empire. In Eastern and Central Europe the internal empire was made up of a chain of federal republics (Estonia, Latvia, Lithuania, Byelorussia, Ukraine, Moldavia) which extended from the Baltic to the Black Sea as a protective band for the Russian central nucleus (RSFSR). The external empire was made up of countries which had adhered to the Warsaw Pact and to COMECON: small, mono-national or multi-national satellite-states, which allowed Soviet domination to extend to Berlin, Prague, Dresden, and Budapest, in the heartland of the previous imperial rivals of Russia. In the internal empire, as in the external one, ruling classes, military leaders, and official intellectuals were picked and controlled on the basis of rigid adherence to an ideology with a remarkable power of cohesion, whose overt nationalism promised to keep under control areas dense with national aspirations and potential ethnic conflicts.

This empire at one point controlled more than 6,430,000 km$^2$—almost 62% of the European continent. But even in the first few years after the war, along with the Soviet expansionist power the first weaknesses and limits began to show. The Soviet Union still did not achieve what was one of the constant—and constantly frustrated—objectives of the Czarist Empire: access to the Mediterranean. In the early fifties, Greece and Turkey came down in favor of the Western bloc, and became integral parts of the Atlantic alliance. Nor did the Soviet Union manage to find a steady outlet on the Adriatic, through ports of great strategic importance such as the Bay of Kotor and Valona. Even before the end of the war, Yugoslavia and Albania had adopted a Soviet-style regime. But soon enough—even though they remained faithful to socialist economies and ideologies—they freed themselves from the Soviet bloc to seek different foreign relations.

The limits that Soviet expansionism found in the Balkans were not the only ones. West Berlin—western outpost in the external empire—was defended by area and remained standing. And Germany as a whole was not neutralized: on the contrary, the biggest part of it was integrated into the Western Alliance. Austria and Finland also did not make it into the Soviet bloc. Militarily neutral, they joined the Western Economic Association.

In the long run, in was the limits experienced in the external empire which proved more significant. The attraction the Soviet regime was capable of exerting on public opinion was quite limited in the years immediately after the war, and disappeared after the complete replication of political and economic systems in what Moscow wanted to turn into a monolithic bloc. The revolts in East Berlin (1953) and Budapest (1956) left no doubt as to the new order's unpopularity.

The following decades saw the success of the Western countries: postwar reconstruction, economic development, integration processes at various levels, loosened restrictions between borders, and the almost complete disappearance of national conflicts. Discussions of the decline of Europe became unfashionable. Although subordinated to the bipolarism of the blocs, Western Europe found its place again in the global economy and geopolitics.

If the two previous European orders had collapsed with the two World Wars, 1989–1990 led to the surprise of a historical discontinuity, which happened by almost completely peaceful means.

Two dates seem to us to capture the extent of this change.

On the sixteenth of June 1989, two hundred thousand people gathered in Budapest to mourn Imre Nagy, the Hungarian head of state during the anti-Soviet revolt of 1956. With this step, the peoples of Central and Eastern Europe began to thaw their memories, overthrew official history, and began to write their own counter-history. Those branded as traitors became heroes to be placed next to the other protagonists of national history. The political and economic reforms were accompanied by a jump-start in the social imagination.

On the third of October, the date of German reunification—a state border that had been hermetically sealed for decades disappeared. The border had no ethnic or deep historical reasons, but was the mark of limited sovereignty, of the protectorate which all Central and Eastern Europe had been subjected to. Now, it was once again the people of the region themselves who had become the arbiters of their own destiny.

The countries of Western Europe went from being peripheral to becoming magnets for the whole continent. A great majority of the states, which had in the preceding decades been members of COMECON and the Warsaw Pact, clearly expressed their desire to become part of the European Union and other European networks. In very little time, the request for economic integration was followed by a request for military integration. The loosening of borders, the birth of new trans-national communities—was this going to be the destiny of the whole continent?

On June 25th, 1991, Slovenia and Croatia, two republics of the Yugoslav federation—unilaterally proclaimed their independence, declaring irreconcilable the conflict of interests and values between them and a third republic in the federation: Serbia. In one fell swoop, two new nation-states and two new borders were born.

Since the Second World War, there had been no open conflict between European nation-states.

On June 27, 1991, the army of the dying Yugoslav federation took up arms to try to stop or limit the effect of Slovenian secession. Its attempt was a failure. Slovenian independence was not questioned any more.

But the cruel skirmishes became an atrocious tragedy when, a few days later, the Yugoslavian army intervened against Croatia, with the pretext of defending the rights of Serb populations in certain regions. Slowly but surely, the image and nature of the war changed. From a war of secession between the Yugoslavian federal army and a federal state, the conflict became one between two absolute and sovereign states: Croatia and "small Yugoslavia" (Serbia and Montenegro), which had defined itself the heir of the defunct federation. Above all, the conflict became total, dragging civilian populations along with it into the abyss.

War has suddenly returned to Europe precisely in the moment when internal peace in our continent seemed assured. At the end of 1990—with the dissolution of the blocs—none of the sovereign states of Europe showed any hostile intentions towards neighboring states.

Europe has begun questioning itself again about the fairness of borders, about ethnic conflict. History—with its ambiguities, risks, and possibilities, its horrors and its conquests—has become a protagonist once again. The future has become uncertain.

In the summer of 1991, the rapid independence of Slovenia was guaranteed also—and above all—by the fact that the new border between Slovenia and Croatia was an ethnic border, which did not present any big problems of minorities on either side of the border. Between Croatia and what was left of Yugoslavia—on the other hand—things were very different. In almost all the border regions there were strong nuclei of Serbian population—majorities in some communities, minorities in others—and they rapidly began to show their opposition to the new Croatian institutions. While the Croatians were preparing their secession from a Yugoslavia which threatened to become a large Serbia, the inhabitants of small Serbias by the borders in turn prepared their secession from what they perceived to be a large Croatia, which was foreign to them.

In nearby Bosnia-Herzegovina, not two, but three peoples lived side by side. In 1991, the region counted 43.7% Moslems, 31.4% Orthodox (Serbs), 17.3% Catholics (Croats). Another 5.5% simply declared itself Yugoslavian: in general this was a sign of an awareness of roots and mixed origins.

Just like 80 years earlier, no ethnicity had a real majority. But, most importantly, this complex mixture applied also to the most restricted territories, all the way down to individual communities. In all of Bosnia-Herzegovina, out of 103 communities, only 27 had a definite, single, ethnic majority (over 75%): 10 with a Croatian majority, 9 with a Serbian majority, and 8 with a Moslem majority. The others were either bi-polar (Moslem-Serb, Serb-Moslem, Moslem-Croat, Croat-Moslem, Serb-Croat, Croat-Serb) or tri-polar.

In 1914, Gavrilo Princip's pistol-shot marked, symbolically, a deadly clash between the ancient multi-national empires and the new nation-states.

In 1992, our century's turmoil has led us back to a clash between "multi-national" and "mono-national," but with grave and important differences. The attackers are the new nation-states of the Serbs and the Croatians: states that had already been ethnically "purified," were even more hardened, and denied coexistence on their land for all southern Slavs, and particularly among Catholics and Orthodox, which in 1914 had still seemed a desirable objective. Only the territory of Bosnia-Herzegovina defends itself as a multi-national state. But little by little, there remains only one ethnic community defending itself: the Moslems, who, unlike the Serbs and Croats, do not have an external territory as a reference point.

Europe and the United States also seem stunned by the idea of a partition. With successive articulations of their peace plans, they only insist that the division be "fair." But how can a division be "fair" when it is imposed on an area in which the mixture of people extends all the way down to communities themselves, in which subdivisions and villages are made up of divergent ethnic groups? How can a division be fair when it imposes the negation of the roots of individuals and communities, the denial of history and memory? At best, the invitation towards division has been an invitation to migration, to deportation, to engage in forced exchanges of populations. At worst, it has been heard as a call for ethnic cleansing, in the most extreme and atrocious sense.

In the centuries of the Modern Age, Sarajevo and Bosnia-Herzegovina have belonged to two great multi-national empires which dominated vast regions of Europe. They were the Ottoman empire from 1463 to 1878, and the Austro-Hungarian empire from 1878 to 1918.

Twice, in Sarajevo and Bosnia-Herzegovina, processes were started which led to the collapse of empires.

In 1875, the poor farmers of Bosnia, both Christian and Moslem, arose against the oppression they were held in by great land owners, of Slav origin, but Moslem by religion, and whose conservatism led to them being known as "more Turkish than the Turks." Within two years, a game of actions and reactions was to lead the Russian Empire to declare war on the Ottoman Empire, fueling an inevitable decline.

In 1914, Gavrilo Princip's pistol shot changed the destiny not just of the Habsburg Empire but of all of Europe.

In our century, Sarajevo and Bosnia have twice belonged to multinational states which wanted to weave together the stories of many peoples.

In 1918, they became part of the kingdom of the Serbs, Croats, and Slovenians.

In 1945, they became part of the socialist federal republic of Yugoslavia.

Twice they saw the compromises, the equilibria, the failures and mistakes of these states. Twice they saw internal tensions, in completely different Europes, come to a head: in 1941 and in 1991.

In the last one hundred years—around Sarajevo and Bosnia—in all the Balkans, there has been a circle of states seeking to become one nation. All these states have internally practiced one form or another of "cleansing." All these states have had to defend themselves from many external enemies, near and far. All these states have laboriously built or transformed their identity, sometimes at the expense of the other states, but sometimes also at their own expense.

In Sarajevo and in Bosnia, the ethnic equilibrium has miraculously been conserved, among all the ethnic and religious tensions after all the tragedies of a century. It has broken only at the end of the century, when the crises seemed to have become remote. And when it did break, it did so with such frightful atrocity that all the tragedies and all the crises came flooding back into memory all at once.

There is too much history today in the memory of Europeans. But this tormented territory must nevertheless be crossed.

In our century—in Sarajevo, in Bosnia, in the Balkans—wars have been fought over multi-national empires, multi-national states (centralized and federal), and mono-national states. None has come out the winner. All have ended up exhausted. The participants have left behind them ruin and barbarism. They have destroyed solidarity and networks of coexistence. They have turned against history, against the identity and the daily life of populations.

Confronted with the inviolability of all the orders that were tried out on Balkan soil for over a century, all of Europe is forced to look at itself, and to take charge of its own history and its identity. In particular, Europe is pushed towards questioning an unspoken assumption of its recent history: that the definitive institutional form adopted by the collectivity and by the European people should be the absolute and sovereign state, which recognizes no authority beyond itself, and strictly subordinates all the authorities that are a part of it.

# 3

## The roots of Europe

### The original ruptures and syntheses

The present condition of Europe owes a lot to an extremely ancient border, which separates Catholic and Protestant peoples from Orthodox peoples; peoples who have for centuries had Latin as their language of culture and peoples who for centuries had Greek as their language of culture; peoples who had Rome as the center of their civilization from peoples who had first Constantinople, and then, at times, Moscow as the center of their civilization.

This border dates back to A.D. 395.

In that year, the emperor Theodosius was succeeded by his two sons, Arcadius and Honorius: the first one was awarded the administration of the Eastern part of the empire, the second was awarded the western part of the empire.

In the preceding century, this sort of division had been frequent. It had never stopped the empire from remaining one, and the attitude of the people toward the empire's authority had not changed.

For at least two centuries, many tribes (particularly of Germanic stock) were pushing on the borders of the empire. Armed incursions were not unusual. And just as common was the peaceful establishment of new populations inside the borders, as settlers. Many men from these populations enlarged the ranks of the imperial armies.

The event which precipitated the situation was the appearance of a new wave of invaders, who came from very far away. They were the Huns: Asiatic nomads of Turkish stock, mixed with other ethnic branches (Mongols, Hungarian-Finnish, Tungus). They were the distant descendants of the Hsiung-nu, who for many centuries had been the dangerous enemies of the Chinese empires. Advancing through the plains between the Dnepr and the Carpathians, they terrorized Gothic, Iranian, and Slavic peoples in their way. These peoples then turned their migrations to within the Roman

Empire's borders. It set off a chain reaction which was to continue for many centuries.

The Greek half of the empire managed to avert the great tide which crashed onto the Latin world. As a consequence, classical Greek culture, even though transformed by Christianity, survived in the East for many centuries. In the West, on the other hand, the sudden and extensive irruption of Germanic people was the origin of new syntheses, which were to initiate a new age of history.

What, in 395, was a purely administrative limit in the vicinity of the Adriatic coast was consolidated, and became a cultural and spiritual limit, until it extended throughout the continent. In the process of evangelization, Croats, Hungarians, the western Slavs, (Czechs, Slovaks, Poles), Baltic peoples (Lithuanians and Letts), Estonians and Finns, were all reached by Roman Christianity, while most of the southern Slavs (Serbs, Bulgarians, Macedonians, Montenegrins), Rumanians, and eastern Slavs (Russians, Ukrainians, Byelorussians) were reached by Greek Christianity.

Over the centuries, the border created conflicts. Originally, the Slavs of Bohemia and Moravia were reached and converted to Christianity by Saints Cyril and Methodius, who had left for the East and translated the scriptures into the Slavonic dialect of the region of Salonika (Slavo-Macedonian). But their work received a hostile reaction from Rome and competition from the Western bishops. In the end, Latin Christendom won a victory over Greek Christendom: Bohemia and Moravia were integrated into the bishops' network. Precisely the opposite occurred in the conversion of the Bulgarian people: Constantinople vigorously intervened to prevent the possibility of a western apostasy.

More than two centuries after the division of the two imperial worlds, a second fracture line developed.

Nomadic Arabs broke onto the scene in the Middle East with a new faith which had recently conquered and unified them: Islam. In the same year (636) they inflicted a mortal defeat on the Sassanid dynasty—which ruled the Persian empire—and then, defeating the armies of the Byzantine empire, opened the doors towards Palestine and Sinai. For the Arabs and for Islam, two directions outlined themselves. In the short span of one century, the eastern route led to Mesopotamia, the valleys of the southern Caucasus, the shores of the Caspian sea, the Iranian plateau, the oases and steppes of Central Asia, and the Indus valley. The western route brought them to Egypt,

Libya, the countries of Northern Africa (from then on known as Maghreb, or west), and, finally, on the European continent, the Iberian peninsula.

The two fractures started to separate the heirs of the Latin civilization from different adjacent cultural worlds: a Near East (from the Balkans to Anatolia), a Middle East (which included the southern and eastern coasts of the Mediterranean, where Islam had found great success), the Far East (characterized by the presence and vitality of ancient religions: Hinduism, Buddhism, Taoism). Of course, this perspective was and is Euro-centric: the differences between the civilizations within the East are probably greater than those internal to the world dominated by the three monotheistic religions.

The events of 395 and 636 certainly did not constitute definitive thresholds, nor did they create irrevocable barriers. Rather, together they opened a vast number of possibilities. In the following centuries, the Latin, Greek, and Islamic elements stimulated each other, and their cross-pollinations contributed substantially in outlining what was later to become Europe.

As far as the relations between the Latin and Greek worlds was concerned, it is important to remember that the end of the empire of Rome, in 476, was not felt by the people of the day to be a lessening of imperial authority on the Western provinces. On the contrary, the rulers of the new German kingdoms, who in the fifth century transformed the face of the ancient Western half of the empire, tended to seek legitimacy from the throne in Constantinople. And it is precisely as representative of the imperial power that Theodoric, king of the Ostrogoths, was able to create a vast dominion in Italy and the surrounding regions.

This legitimacy was an important instrument for the Emperor Justinian, when at the beginning of the following century, turning the military situation to his favor, he regained Italy, Spain, and Northern Africa. A part of these conquests proved temporary. But, in the Italian peninsula, the presence of Greek authority and civilization persisted. Venice developed thanks to the Eastern Empire's protection; Bari and Calabria remained in its possession for a few more centuries.

The divergence between the Roman Catholic church and the Orthodox church was not sudden. It was not due to a real schism, but to differences in attitude which in the end produced different worlds. The Eastern Church, backed by an empire with an ancient tradition, was uncomfortable with the Western church's tendency to move out of spiritual circles to get directly involved in political matters. It was also uncomfortable with the subordination of the entire hierarchy to one head, preferring, for its part, to recognize patriarchates that were independent and communicating. The two Churches slowly drifted apart.

On the other hand, Islam's irruption did not interrupt the relations that, in the ancient world, had tied together Europe, the Mediterranean, Asia Minor, the steppes and oases of Central Asia, India, and China. The Arabs did not receive a hostile reception from the Christians they met along their journey. On the contrary, the eastern Christian churches (the Nestorian churches in Mesopotamia, the Jacobite in Syria, the Coptic in Egypt) had become independent of the church in Constantinople the previous century. They had been persecuted by the Empire because of the schism. The new dominators favorably welcomed the Christians among their subjects: they did not attempt to convert them directly, and often protected them. They, nevertheless, put them under strong economic pressure, and in order to escape it many embraced Islam.

The symbiosis between Islam and the Western churches was an important moment in the construction of Western civilization. For Europe, a great part of the knowledge about literature, philosophy, and science of classical Greece was not a direct inheritance. It was inherited through a curious and fecund circle. Greek works were translated into Syrian by Nestorian Christians who lived in Baghdad and surrounding Mesopotamia. There they were translated into Arab, and from there spread throughout the Islamic world, up to its Western extremity, the Iberian peninsula. There, in the Middle Ages, they started becoming known in Latin Christendom....

Other solidarities linked East and West. For centuries, along the silk road, Christianity, Islam, and Buddhism coexisted, and, along with other ancient religions (Manicheism, Zoroastrianism) they reached Turkestan, the Mongol leaders, and the Emperor of China. A flux of ideas going from East to West is documented in the fact that the Sufis, Islamic mystics of the Middle Ages, knew the Indian Yoga systems, and acted as conduits for certain Eastern ideas, which penetrated Europe starting with the Crusades.

Throughout the Middle Ages, two civilizations, the Latin and the Greek, accompanied each other, interwoven, variously superimposed and counterpoised to two higher authorities: the Church and the Empire. With the most disparate results, the game of the four universalisms produced important roots for the states and peoples of today's Europe.

In the East, the coexistence of Church and empire had no continuity. The church followed an empire of ancient and well-rooted juridical and cultural tradition. This made the separation of the spheres easier, and attenuated, even if it did not nullify, the destructive potential of conflicts of authority. The so-called "Caesar-papism," the fact that the Emperor was recognized as the head of the church, and was allowed to legislate on the subject of heresies, was only an apparent subordination of the Church to the Empire. Leaving a vast field for imperial decisions, the Church wanted to ensure for itself the care of the inner and spiritual dimensions.

The situation in the West was much more intricate.

For at least three centuries, from 400 until after 700, the cultural and institutional flowering of the Church of Rome faced the political pulverization and cultural mutation, which impregnated the new kingdoms with Germanic customs and habits. The church felt responsible not only to maintain classical culture, but also to re-establish connections between the territories and recompose relations of authority. Almost all the barbarian kingdoms were not only virtually unlivable, but they were also leading the way to new processes of fragmentation. Many fell immediately to the new external invasions: the reconquest of Justinian, the Islamic invasions, the landing of the Scandinavians.... Others became degraded and tangled in a web of local authorities, precursors of future duchies and principalities.

But one of these kingdoms managed to achieve a first re-composition of the European territory and civilization. It was the kingdom of the Franks, a Germanic people beyond the Rhine, which had place itself at the head of one of the most compact and civilized regions of the ancient empire: Gaul. On their land, the Franks managed to amalgamate Latin and German civilization. And they moved on several fronts, in Latin and German Europe. To the south, they blocked the Arab invaders and went over the borders beyond the Pyrenees, toward Barcelona. In the East and North-East, they subdued many Germanic peoples, even reaching areas with Slavic populations beyond the Elbe.

Between the two major authorities of the day in Europe, the Franks and the papacy, a convergence started to develop, and a complex negotiation. The result was the rebirth of the Western empire, with the crowning of Charlemagne in Rome on December 25th of the year 800.

Europe had found a new center, both spiritual and political, further north than the ancient world. At this point it embraced virtually all of Latin Christianity. It included most of Germany, Gaul, and Italy. Of the countries which made Rome their spiritual authority, it excluded only the British Isles and the small Iberian kingdom of Asturias.

The way in which this re-composition of the center was arrived at was to make a profound mark on the following centuries of European history.

In the Christian-Latin-Germanic world this construction defined a double tension.

A first tension was geographic. The seat of the papacy was in Rome, a central region for the ancient world, but one which had now become peripheral, on the immediate border with Byzantine possessions, and always under the threat of Saracen invasions. The new political center was in Aachen, near the ethnic border between neo-Latin languages (which would give birth to the French language) and Germanic languages (which would give birth to the German language).

A second tension was clearly political. Since the negotiations which traced the new empire, both players, the pope and the new emperor, clearly showed the intention of defining themselves superior to the other. For the chroniclers of the times, the coronation ceremony had a clear winner in the pope, who placed the crown on Charlemagne's head *before* he was proclaimed Emperor by his army, the traditional source of legitimation in Germanic kingdoms. The Emperor naturally did not take the defeat well. The seeds were sown for a millennium-long controversy.

The imperial center, at any rate, fell apart in a few decades. The death sentence appeared in the form of new internal particularisms and new external invasions.

The ascendancy to the imperial throne had not eliminated the practice, common in the kingdom of Franks and other Germanic kingdoms, following which territory was to be considered the personal patrimony of the reigning clan, to be divided between sons, or whoever else had the right of succession. Adherence to this principle created a complicated web of conflicts, which discredited the imperial throne and pulverized the territory of the Franks.

In the ninth and tenth centuries, new actors emerged on the European scene.

The Normans, Germanic peoples from Scandinavia, made a series of maritime expeditions and raids. They kept under their domain a good deal of the British isles. They settled in distant Iceland. They spread terror along the French coast, from the Channel to the Atlantic. Often they went up rivers and looted cities: they traveled up the Seine to Paris, and along the Loire to Orléans. With great audacity, they moved into the Mediterranean, reaching Marseilles and the Italian port of Luni.

The Islamic Saracens, for their part, had a firm grip on the Western Mediterranean isles (Malta, Sicily, the Balearic Islands), and from their bases devastated the nearby coasts.

In 895, the Hungarians (Magyars), nomadic tribes of Hungarian-Finnish stock with Turkish influences, came down to the Pannonian plain between the Danube and the Tisa from the steppes of the Volga and the Black Sea. From this location, they engaged in a series of raids over considerable ground, spreading death and destruction in Germany and Italy. Only after a century did they finally settle in Pannonia, in the territory that to this day is occupied by their descendants.

The insecurity of the times was such that people sensed all the weight of a great historical discontinuity. It was only then that the call of Latin culture and roots was interrupted completely. It was only then that the Middle Ages started.

# 4

## A thousand years ago

### The story of a new Europe

The two "dark centuries" left a decisive heritage. Around the year 1000, a new Europe emerged, with clearly defined ethnic characteristics. They were to have an impact on all the following centuries.

A thousand years ago, a pattern emerged in the European population which, in its deepest form, is with us to this day.

The eight preceding centuries had seen the movement of peoples from Central and Eastern Europe towards North and South (numberless Germanic and Slavic tribes); from Scandinavia towards Central Europe and East-Central Europe (Normans and Vikings: Germanic peoples of the "second wave"); from the Urals, from the forests of Siberia and the steppes of Central Asia towards the valley of the Volga, the coast of the Black Sea, the Baltic Sea, and Central Europe (Ugro-Finnic and Turko-Mongolian peoples: Hungarians, Finns, Avars, Bulgarians, Khazars); even from remote Arabia to the Western, Southern, and Eastern coasts of the Mediterranean and some of its islands.

At the end of those eight centuries, the heart of Europe was solidly in the hands of three of the great stocks (or "linguistic branches") in which the Indo-European populations had divided themselves in the preceding millennia. It was the stocks of the Latins, the Germans, and the Slavs (Baltic-Slavs, more precisely), which began a game of equilibrium and reciprocal containment.

Under pressure from the Germanic peoples, the Latin civilization had to abandon Great Britain and the region by the Rhine, and all the Germanic peoples who had penetrated into Gaul and the Iberian peninsula became Latinized.

Equally unstable were the borders between Germans and Slavs. In the beginning, it was the Slavs who prevailed: from the East they pushed all the way to the Elbe, to the Alps, up to the higher Danube, in regions that today belong to Mecklenburg, Brandenburg, Austria, and Bavaria. Immediately afterwards, a slow and constant Germanic counter-push towards the East developed. Around 1000, the Germans were involved in the colonization of the vast space between the Elbe and the Oder. This enterprise was progressively crowned with success: for the Germans it became the springboard for their attempt to establish themselves in regions even further east, in the space between the Oder and the Vistula, and on the Eastern and South-Eastern coast of the Baltic. But this push eastward (*Drang nach Osten*) found its limit and containment in the resistance of peoples in whom the Slav world was beginning to fragment (Czechs, Poles, Sorbs, Kashubians) and their immediate relatives, the Baltic peoples (Lithuanians, Letts). In those centuries, the basis was created for a movable border between Germans and Slavs, a breakpoint but also a place of connection, which was to mark many phases of European history.

Faced with the blossoming of these three great Indo-European stocks, others stocks were to contract or crystallize.

The Celtic stock disappeared from continental Europe, although it had been a majority in many regions. The Celtic languages remained, for centuries, flourishing in the western part of the British Isles, and they even managed to settle in a region of the European continent (the peninsula of Brittany), but nevertheless they began to retreat in front of the Anglo-Saxon, and later English, onslaught.

The Greek language started to lose ground: following the expansion of the Slavs in the Balkans and the Arabs in the Middle East (to which was added, in 1050 and 1450, the arrival of the Turks in the Anatolian peninsula), it found itself restricted to its place of origin, the peninsula of Hellas and the Aegean islands, even though it remained an important language for communication and culture for the Orthodox East and the whole of Europe.

The Illyrian stock almost completely disappeared from the Balkans, generating only one people of modern Europe: the Albanians.

The Iranic populations (belonging to the western branch of that Indo-Iranic stock that today in Asia counts many hundreds of millions) abandoned the plains of the Ukraine and Southern Russia, which they dominated until the first centuries of our era (Scythians, Sarmatae, Alans): they left as their only descendants the language, culture, and population of the Ossetians, today divided between Russia and Georgia, in the valley of the Caucasus.

In the first thousand years of our era, other linguistic and ethnic events transformed Europe.

The ancient non-Indo-European languages (which we might call pre-Indo-European, because heirs of extremely distant lines of our continent's population) remained only in peripheral areas: Basque, in the mountains of the Pyrenees; Georgian and many other "Caucasian" tongues, in the mountains between Russia and Asia Minor.

Other languages disappeared without a trace, as was the case with the language of the Picts, a people of extremely ancient and obscure origin, which was still dominant in Scotland in the fifth century BC.

Above all, what became the new (tripartite) ethnic nucleus of Europe (Neo-Latin, Germans, Baltic-Slavs), managed an effective containment and integration of the new wave of peoples coming from Asia. Peoples of Hungarian-Finnish origin, whose original home was probably in the Urals and Western Siberia, settled along the Volga (Mordvinians), in the Pannonian plain between the Danube and the Tisa (Hungarians), along the Western banks of the Baltic (Finns, Estonian, Livonians), and in the great Scandinavian North (Laplanders). But they did not create areas with very extensive and compact populations, because they were interrupted by the expansion of Eastern Slavs (Russians, Ukrainians, Byelorussians). Immediately to the South, numerous tribes of Turkish origin settled along the Volga, in the Western Caucasus, in Crimea, creating the first centers of the populations that are there to this day. Farther West, towards the Danube and the Balkans, their incursions led to the birth of new peoples, through the fusion of the identity of the recent arrivals with the identity of those who had settled there earlier. The genealogical tree of today's Bulgarians goes back to a Slavic stock (from which they got their language), a Turkish stock (which gave them their name), and the ancient stock of the Thracians who lived in the Balkans in the days of the Roman empire. As for the Arab peoples, if their contributions to the civilization of Southern Europe was intense, their ethnic and linguistic contribution was more sporadic: in the Spanish language there remain many words, many geographic names, some phonemes.

After the year 1,000, the new ethnic nucleus of Europe had to endure two further crises, generated from the depths of the Asian continent: the appearance of a new branch of Turks in the Anatolian peninsula and the incursion of the Mongols from the steppes on the margins of China. These crises were also contained. To be sure, in a few centuries the Turks would have forced back the area of Greek language and culture considerably, and would themselves enter the European scene: but the area of their population would not extend beyond the South-Eastern borders of the continent. As for the Mongols, they did not arrive in great numbers, and soon fused with the Turkish populations of Southern Russia: today's Tartars, Bashkirs, and Chuvash are the heirs of this story. Only one Mongolian people has remained in a peripheral corner of the European continent: the Kalmucks, who since the beginnings of the Modern Age have settled on the Western coasts of the Black Sea, the last echo of an era of great movements.

A thousand years ago, in this Europe, which was beginning to stabilize itself, there were born the centers of the future states of Germany and France, and the French and German ethnic identities started defining themselves. The center of European Christianity, the Frankish kingdom, split into a Western and an Eastern half. This schism was both geographic and ethnic. In the West, in the hybridization and integration of Latin and German elements, the Latin element prevailed. In the East, the opposite occurred. It is interesting to note how the most ancient evidence of the French language (indeed, of all neo-Latin languages) is contained in a text that refers precisely to this division of the empire into two parts, namely the Oaths of Strasbourg of 842, with which Charles the Bald, lord of the Western part of the empire, allied himself with his brother Ludwig, lord of Bavaria, to fight his older brother Lothar. Each spoke the oath in the language prevailing among the ally's troops: a sign of a clearly established linguistic border.

The fragmentation of royal power immediately left a space for the birth of other political entities in the intermediate geographical space: Italy, Provençe, Bourgogne, and Lorraine (in German *Lothringen*, from Lothar), a thin strip of land which originally stretched from Alsace to the North Sea, through Flanders.

The collision for possession of the intermediate territories by the two halves, neo-Latin and Germanic, was immediate. Initially, it seemed that the East would prevail. It was Otto, king of Germany, who in 962 convinced the Pope to repeat in Rome the imperial coronation ceremony. It was the king of Germany who took on the heavy task of confronting the continuing diatribes with the papacy to define the supreme authority. It was the king of Germany who undertook interminable expeditions to control Italy and Bourgogne. It was the king of Germany who tried to have his supremacy recognized— purely along theoretical lines—by the other Christian monarchs.

For the moment, the king of Germany also had the task of ensuring the victorious expansion of Christianity towards the east, since the new empire there bordered with Slavic people who were still partly pagan. Along this margin a number of marches were created: border territories of conquest and colonization. The western marches extended the German ethnicity, at the expense of the Slavs, from the Elbe to the Oder. The southern marches (Austria, Styria, Carinthia, Carniola) extended the German ethnicity to the Pannonian plain, where the Magyars had settled, separated the southern Slavs from the western Slavs, creating an ethnic border which has lasted to this day. Between the Elbe and Austria, the western empire incorporated a Slavic kingdom which had enjoyed a transitory independence: the kingdom of Bohemia and Moravia, populated by Czechs, which was to tie its destiny with Germany until 1806, and Austria until 1918.

A thousand years ago, Europe and Latin Christianity enjoyed a considerable expansion. From 925 to 1000 the bases were created for the conversion of those who had been great enemies in previous centuries: the Germans from Jutland and Scandinavia, from whose territories the Norman incursions originated; the Slavs from East of the Oder; the Magyars, now surrounded by Slavs and Germans; other Slavs living in proximity of the Dalmatian coast. The bases were created for the nuclei of the kingdoms of Denmark, Norway, Sweden, Poland, Hungary, and Croatia. Around the imperial nucleus, the outline of a Latin-Germanic-Slavic Christianity was emerging, a spiritual confederation ably supported by the pontiff in Rome. One strategy proved particularly effective in tying ancient enemies to Europe. This was the strategy of downward conversion: the baptism of the king was a prelude to the baptism of the whole population. This strategy could function because in general, for the ethnicities in question, the question of spirituality and cults was strictly tied to the internal cohesion of the group and clan. Loyalty to the ruler, expression of the collectivity, naturally prevailed over individual free choice.

The year 1000 saw both the expansion of Christian universalism and, at the same time, the height of political particularism. In the center of Christian Europe, personal authorities prevailed. The ruler dominated only those spaces and individuals for which he could be physically present. His court was itinerant, and negotiations to assure specific privileges to this or that locale potentate were essential. In the vast kingdoms of the Germans and Franks a pyramidal hierarchy of many levels of authority was created, going from the sovereign ruler to the free castles.

The first two levels of this authority, the sovereign and the princes, were frequently in conflict. The sovereign was elected by the princes in a joint sitting, and was recognized by the princes as a sacred symbol of national unity. But he exercised his authority effectively only on the territories which were hereditary patrimony of the family, the territories he was able to conquer with the sword or with marital allegiances, or over the territories which were in possession by ecclesiastical orders which were particularly protected or favored. In turn, the princes moved as independent authorities, concerned with the maintenance of vast territories with a strong individual identity. In these spaces of multiple negotiations, small and medium territories (duchies, earldoms, ecclesiastical possessions, rural cantons, even free castles) managed to enjoy long periods of independence. In the following centuries, the destiny of cities was a particularly happy one. In the Low Countries, in Northern Italy, on the Baltic coast, they negotiated a strong autonomy from the imperial power, allowing them great economic development.

At the beginning of the new millennium, the king of Germany, symbolic authority of the imperial power, seemed better able to guarantee the overall unity of his territory than the king of France. The authority of Hugh Capet, initiator of the new dynasty which had inherited the neo-Latin part of the empire, was minimal: a few territories scattered through northern France, around Paris, Orléans, Compiègne. Great regional powers dominated the scene: Aquitaine, Gascony, Brittany, Flanders, Champagne, the western part of Burgundy which did not belong to the imperial territories. Some descendants of the Normans, who had spread so much terror in previous centuries, definitively settled on French soil and recognized royal authority. They received a Duchy in the prosperous region of the Channel, which to this day bears their name.

In 1066, the tables were turned once more. The Duke of Normandy disembarked with his troops beyond the Channel, and became king of another emerging state, England. The descendants of Germanic peoples, who in previous centuries had dominated British soil, (Angles, Saxons, Jutes, Danes, Norwegians) were thrown into the Latin orbit by another people with ancient Germanic roots. On paper, the English king was a vassal of the French king. But this relationship was more inconvenient for the supreme authority than for the subordinate. In the span of a century, interwoven heredities and weddings made the king of England master of almost half of France. Between England and France began centuries of fights, which contributed to forging and strengthening the respective national identities.

In the first centuries of the new millennium, the kings of France became involved in a long reconquest, which, gradually, transformed their nominal possessions from a feudal mosaic into a centralized state. They established precise rules of succession, effectively making the dynasty hereditary. They linked and extended their distant possessions, and organized a stable central capital: Paris. They used every occasion to reaffirm their authority over the nobles, and opened the road to Languedoc, on the Mediterranean coast.

One location and date remain symbolic of this reconquest: Bouvines and 1214. France defeated a coalition comprised of the German emperor, England, and many regional princes. He not only extended his territories, but was now unconstrained by imperial universalism. Thus began the absolute monarchy: jurists defined the king of France as *princeps in regno suo*, or even *imperator in regno suo*. France and Germany were again in equilibrium.

Early in the new millennium, Latin Christianity continued to expand. Around 1200 Christianization of the Scandinavians was complete. Southern Italy (Apulia and Calabria) was re-taken from the Byzantines; Sicily was taken from the Saracens. In the Iberian peninsula, the Christian kingdoms, which around 1000 had been confined to the extreme northern regions (Asturias, León, Navarra, Aragon), expanded towards the center and south and overturned power relations with the Islamic world. After 1250, the Moslems were, in turn, confined to Granada, in the South-eastern corner of Iberia.

The resistance of the pagan populations on the coasts of the Baltic sea was particularly tenacious. The Lithuanians repelled many attempts to subdue them. Their king, Jagiello, converted only when, in exchange, he was promised the crown of the kingdom of Poland. It was 1386. Europe was on the verge of belonging entirely to one faith.

The "fabrication of Europe," to quote William Bartlett, occurred under the sign of homogenization and the replication of identical forms of life, social relations, techniques of agricultural, elements of material culture and the spiritual imaginary. Precisely for this reason, the lands of the ancient Celtic Christianity were forced into submission, since they were out of step with the customs, civilization, and exploitation projects of the expanding center. In some regions, the expansion of Latin Christianity followed the strategy of conversion from above—the conversion of the sovereign, followed by the conversion of the general population. Elsewhere, the expansion was a real process of colonization. Frontier areas were defined, considered virgin territory destined for invasion, division, and settlement. Colonizers were summoned from all over Europe, and the bishops made impassioned pleas to promote the crusades. This happened in southern Spain, and also in the Celtic countries. On the coast of the Baltic, the crusading zeal of the Germanic Teutonic Order victimized an entire ethnicity. The Prussians, a population with ties to present-day Letts and Lithuanians, were decimated and disappeared from history leaving us with few traces of their language.

Western Christianity tried to export its replicating and homogenizing mechanisms (tested in its immediate environments) in the most distant places, at the expense of the most ancient and solid civilizations. Against the Arabs, in the Holy Land, in Palestine, and on the Eastern coast of the Mediterranean, the results were ephemeral. After two centuries, all the Christian kingdoms in the region were re-absorbed, even if the cultural and commercial contacts established during that time proved to be fecund and long-lasting, and even if Christianity had a new impulse in the Syrian-Lebanese coast, which still lasts in our century.

In 1204, the Western crusades made Constantinople rather than Palestine their route. The Byzantine Empire and Orthodox Christianity were reduced to lands of conquest, when formerly they had been on an equal footing with the Western Empire. The looting of Constantinople worked. The violence of the Crusaders made the incursions of Islamic Saracens almost pale in comparison. In the city, the Latin ecclesiastical hierarchy replaced the Greek one. Ephemeral Latin principalities were born: Morea (the Peloponnesus) went to the French. An Italian city-state, Venice, gained conspicuous commercial advantage from the new order in the Near East. In the following decades, precisely in regions that formerly belonged to the ancient Eastern empire, the nuclei of two more regions of modern Europe: the region of the Slavs and the region of the Bulgarians, people of Slav language and Orthodox religion.

In the long term, the surprise attack of 1204 proved to be damaging both for the victors and the vanquished. The Byzantines soon recaptured Constantinople. But the Empire of the East was never to be the same, surviving for another two centuries with ever-diminishing territories. The space this civilization occupied was not taken over by Western Christianity, but by a new Islamic power. Originating in remote provinces of Asia, the Ottoman Turks spread throughout Anatolia, and made their first appearance on European soil. Their ascent swept away everything in its path: residues of the Greek dominion, Latin principalities, the Venetian commercial empire.

The independence of the Serbs and Bulgarians was also short-lived. Their kingdoms were also involved in the Westward expansion of the Ottoman Turks, despite a tenacious fight which left an indelible imprint in Balkan folklore and literature. One of the crucial episodes of this fight, the battle between Serbs and Turks on the field of the Kosovo on June 28 1389, remain indelibly in the memory and national identity of the Serb people. But, at the time, for the Balkan Christians, the only choice seemed to be to head for the mountains or the forests. Many communities transferred *en masse* to inaccessible regions, with the pope at their head.

Immediately after 1200, further destructive events occurred between Europe and Asia. More barriers were raised between the civilizations. Western India was invaded by Turko-Afghani peoples. They destroyed cultural and spiritual patrimonies of inestimable value, and almost eliminated Buddhism from its land of origin, forcing it to become an exiled religion. The whole of Central Asia, the Iranic plateau, Mesopotamia, the Caucasus, the steppes of the Ukraine, of the Volga, and of Southern Siberia were overtaken by a new wave of invading nomads, originating from the depths of the Asian continent: the Mongols.

In the following century, from 1308 to 1405, the Islamic and Christian Middle East (Mesopotamia, Iran, Caucasus, Anatolia), was forced to undergo an even more terrifying ordeal: the invasion, starting in Samarkand, of new Turko-Mongol hordes, led by Tamarlain. The massacres perpetrated in at that time were such that previously fertile regions were transformed into arid and desolate steppes, and reduced, noticeably and irreversibly, the number of faithful belonging to the Christian churches of the West. From that moment on, their essentially intermediary role between East and West began to diminish.

The last series of events which raised the barrier between West and East, between Christianity and Islam, and which remains to this day, occurred on European soil, in 1492. At the beginning of that year, the monarchs of a new Christian kingdom, Spain, ended the kingdom of Granada, the last remaining Muslim state in the Iberian Peninsula. A few months later, the same monarchs published a decree, which ordered the approximately 300,000 Spanish Jews to convert or leave, and confiscated the belongings of those who chose to emigrate. Many decided to leave nevertheless, developing a difficult Diaspora throughout the Mediterranean basin. From that point onward, Spain recognized only one religious faith.

# 5

## 1453/1648

### Between universalisms and monarchies

In 1453, Constantinople was definitively conquered by the Ottoman Turks. It was the end of the eastern empire. The order of the Balkans, and of the whole of south-east Europe, was inverted. A hundred years of tremendous change began for Europe and the world. A new age had begun: the Modern Age.

A claim was made on the heritage of the eastern empire. Ivan III, Prince of Moscow, crowned his supremacy over the other Russian cities (in 1472) by marrying Zoe Paleologo, one of the last descendants of the imperial family, and obtained the title of Caesar (*Czar/Zar*). Between Europe and Asia a new empire was born which wanted to move the center of Orthodox Christianity, now that Constantinople was under Islamic rule. To make Moscow worthy of being "the third Rome," the Czar had a fortress (*Kreml'*) built in the center of the city, which contained a complex network of splendid palaces and magnificent churches. In 1480, the Russia declared itself free from obedience and vassalage to the Khanate of the Golden Horde (the Turko-Mongolian state, which, for over two centuries, had dominated all plains of southern Russia).

Initially, the new empire expanded eastward. The western Urals were reached and traversed in the last twenty years of the fifteenth century. The peoples who lived there (Komi, Khanty, Vogul, Samoyed) were enslaved and, at times, decimated. In the sixteenth century, a series of battles broke out between the Turko-Mongol khanates that remained on European territory. The new Czar, Ivan IV (the "Terrible"), used the opportunity to conquer the length of the Volga, from Kazan, to eastern Moscow, all the way to Astrakhan on the Caspian Sea. By the end of the sixteenth century, the Czarist domain extended for the length of the Ob: it was a promising chain of forward position to push farther inside the Asian continent.

The ancient imperial capital, Constantinople, (now Istanbul), saw settlement and metamorphosis. Already Islamicized at the time of their settlement in Central Asia and Persia, in the previous centuries the Ottomans had gone from nomads to being sedentary, and had made their roots in the Anatolian peninsula, thousands of kilometers west of their place of origin (south-central Siberia). Now, they had experienced a further transformation: from an Asian power they had become a Eurasian power. They presided over an ethnic mosaic, in which Islamic populations lived with many Christian faiths (Orthodox, Catholic, Armenian, Jacobite, Coptic, etc.) and with sizable, expanding Jewish centers.

The Ottoman order was certainly filled with the memory of the original warrior hordes and the idea of the supremacy of the Islamic faith. A clear distinction was made between *Moslem* (believers) and *zimmî* (non-Muslim "protected"). The new Turkish rulers also wanted to become the preservers of the civilization of Constantinople and its ethnic and cultural world. It was precisely for this reason that they reserved the right to ratify the nomination of the Greek Patriarch of Constantinople, who continued to enjoy the status and privileges he had in the empire. The Ottomans did not seek to Turkicize or Islamicize the empire. On the contrary, the ethnic settlements of Turks and other Islamic populations (Tartars, Turkmen, Circassians) were concentrated in the capital, in strategic areas, or in sparsely populated areas of the plains or coasts. Around 1530, the population of the Balkans continued to be 80% Christian, against 19% Moslem and 1% Jewish.

The Ottomans governed the non-Islamic ethnicities with the interposition of vassal states (Wallachia, Moldavia, Transylvania, the Republic of Ragusa) and, above all, as far as the subject populations were concerned, the system of *millet* (religious communities). Three were recognized: the Jewish, the Armenian (the Armenians had had a Monophysite national church since the fifth century), and the Greek (to which all Orthodox Christians belonged). Every millet had the autonomy to govern over the religious and moral sphere. In practice, this involved issues regarding family, education, and assistance to the sick and old. Nevertheless, there were frequent conflicts of competency with Islamic law, which governed the empire as a whole. Heading the Greek millet was the Patriarch of Constantinople, who exercised his jurisdiction over multiple and disparate ethnicities (Greeks, Bulgarians, Serbs, Albanians, Wallachians...). The fact that these communities were conceived only in religious terms, but not also in ethnic/linguistic terms was to have great importance for the future of the Balkans.

In the first decades of the sixteenth century, the Ottoman Turks undertook a new expansion, which led them to spread through the Pannonian plains, control large part of the kingdoms of Croatia and Hungary, and conquer Belgrade. Their advance towards the center of Europe was stopped in Vienna, in 1529. Along their way, the Ottomans encountered a new multinational formation. At the head of it was the dynasty of the German Emperor. By now, the title of emperor belonged to the house of Habsburg. Originating from the upper Rhine, between Alsace, Brisgovia, and Switzerland, in the previous centuries the Habsburgs had acquired marches, counties, and cities at the south-eastern borders of the empire: Austria, Styria, Carinthia, Carniola, Tyrol, Vorarlberg, Istria and Trieste. In the first decades of the sixteenth century, they also added the crowns of the ancient Christian kingdoms of central Europe: Bohemia, Hungary, and Croatia. The Habsburgs had, in this way, become possessors of a vast and compact territory in the very heart of Europe, with a mixed population: Germans (Austria/Tyrol), Slavs (Bohemia/Carniola), Magyars (Hungary), Italians (Trieste). Although great parts of the Kingdoms of Croatia and Hungary were then under Ottoman dominion, their historical rights were in the hands of the Habsburgs, who became the Christian protectors in the Balkans. Now, along the Danube and in the plains of Pannonia, the players were two.

The beginning of the Modern Age was, above all, the time of four monarchies situated at the western margins of the continent: France, England, Spain, and Portugal.

The western monarchies successfully continued or completed national unification, with the absorption or subjugation of ancient regional identities (Navarra, Catalonia, Provençe, Burgundy, Brittany, Scotland, and Ireland). In 1453, France and England ended a long season of wars and reciprocal collisions. From then on, English presence disappeared from the continent. France continued, successfully, the fight against the ancient feudal domains. In 1477, it ended the power of the Duke of Burgundy; in 1488, the duchy of Brittany was annexed. Beyond the Pyrenees, in 1479, the fusion of two large and powerful kingdoms—Castille and Aragon—produced modern Spain.

The monarchies were at the vanguard of what Anthony Smith has called a triple revolution: economic (which brought division of labor, a general system of tax collection, and state monopolies on many kinds of products); centralization (which led to the control and expansion of administration); cultural (which allowed for the birth of a national collective imagination, an educational system, a linguistic and communicative space common to a great number of individuals and collectivities). With the edict of Villers-Cotterêts (1539), the King of France imposed the use of the standardized national language of the chancelleries. This was at the expense not only of the already declining Latin, or of certain French dialects which had blossomed during the Middle Ages. It was, above all, the *langue d'oc*, the Occitanian-Provençal, originating from neo-Latin (but distinct from French), which then began a long decline until it became semi-clandestine.

The western monarchies supported and reaped the benefits of the European outpouring over the whole planet. In 1492 the maritime expedition led by Christopher Columbus left the Spanish port of Palos. Looking for a new route to India, they found instead a huge continent. In 1519, Magellan started his voyage of circumnavigation, which brought humanity face to face with the vastness and diversity of the Earth. Already, at the end of the sixteenth century, large parts of Central and South America were in European hands, along with the Caribbean islands, key ports on the coasts of Africa and the East Indies, and some routes in the Pacific.

The European political panorama was turned upside down. The ancient center (defined by the conflict between Pope and Emperor in the German and Italian territories) was transformed. Instead of being the location of symbolic sovereignty exercised on a periphery extended in many directions, it became a terrain of conquest and the theater of a politics of equilibrium of national powers (which were growing and prospering in its margins).

In the fatal 1492, the first wars broke out for dominion over the mosaic of little states that made up Italy. France and Spain were the main protagonists. In the following decades, the King of France (Francis I) found as his adversary, the Habsburg Charles V. Through a series of circumstances and marriages, Charles accumulated supreme authority over the German Empire, the hereditary possessions of Austria, the territory of the Spanish monarch (including the new American colonies), Flanders and the Low Countries (patrimony from the ancient duchy of Burgundy). It was the greatest dominion a German emperor had ever had. It was also the swan-song of medieval political universalism: after 1556, the destinies of the various parts of Charles V's dominion were, forever, separated. The protagonists of the conflict became single states (France, above all), which sought in central Europe new directions for their expansion. Italy's wars were an anticipation of an interminable series of wars for dominion over the continent.

After 1517, Europe's disintegration was intensified by Luther's reforms. Martin Luther certainly contributed to giving Germans a common written language, which strengthened their sense of belonging to a common culture and nation. But the innumerable states and territories of the empire, immediately divided themselves by faith, on top of which there were innumerable local differences. The Catholic emperor attempted to maintain unity, at the expense of religious freedom. The Protestant alliances, defending their religious choices, contributed substantially to the lessening of the supreme authority's prestige.

Lutheran reform created a new cultural and religious unity in Northern Europe: in Scandinavia and around the Baltic coast. Sweden, Denmark, and several north German states became Lutheran. But the Protestant faith did not long remain united. From the Reformation came several strands of Protestantism: Anglicans, Calvinists, Baptists, Anabaptists, and many other sects, in whose concepts and actions were to be found political, national, social, and spiritual exigencies.

The interweaving of political and religious fronts lead to the devastation of Germany. There were two great cycles of wars. The first cycle ended after the Reformation and concluded in 1555, with the Peace of Augusta. The second cycle, even more dramatic, involved all the European powers, both Catholic and Protestant. It began in 1618, when the Bohemian Protestants revolted against the Catholic emperor; it ended in 1648, with a peace agreement made by the exhausted parties. History remembers it as the Thirty Years War.

In the century of religious wars, old and new protagonists ascended and descended within the European hierarchies. Spain and Portugal kept (and at times increased) their great extra-European empires but started to lose their influence on the continent. In Eastern Central Europe, two states experienced a moment of splendor: Poland and Sweden. In 1569, the Polish state and the Lithuanian state fused into a single body, which extended to the nearby lands populated by Lets, Ukrainians, and Byelorussians: the Poles had Kiev, and for a moment dreamt of conquering Moscow. Sweden went outside of its Scandinavian confines and created the basis for a Baltic Empire, with vanguards on the southern and eastern coasts: Pomerania, Estonia, Ingermanland, and Livonia. But the power of these states was brief. Not only did they clash among themselves, but they dragged Russia back into the game. Until then, Russia had concentrated on protecting itself and expanding in the east.

On the same Baltic shores, a new actor emerged: Prussia. Its destiny as a European power began when the Hohenzollern dynasty unified into one state domains strewn in three distant regions, at the ends of the areas of German population: the small duchies of the Rhine region; Brandenburg, in eastern Germany between the Elbe, the Oder, and Pomerania; and eastern Prussia itself, on the shores of the Baltic between Poland and Lithuania.

During the religious wars, small and original states distinguished and consolidated themselves. In 1648, the final settlement that ended the Thirty Years War, sanctioned the formal independence of both the Swiss Confederation and the United Provinces of the Low Countries. Both represented a model of the state that was different from that prevailing in western Europe: a result of the centralization from above practiced by dynasties and sovereigns.

Switzerland and the Low Countries both resulted from a unification which proceded from the bottom up, rather than top down. They burst out of the alliance of small entities (cantons or provinces), that were regional, sub-regional, rural, or cities, and elaborated rules of coexistence to ensure the prevalence of one or more majority entities over all the others. Both Switzerland and the Low Countries guaranteed the stable coexistence of Catholics and Protestants. Religious diversity was maintained and did not disintegrate in the weaving together of the new states.

At the conclusion of the Thirty Years War, many states claimed victory for small political or territorial advantages. In any case, the great losers were the two actors who for many centuries had made Europe the scene of their conflictual cooperation, or their cooperative conflict: the German Empire and the papacy.

The empire was reduced to a mosaic of innumerable feudal and semi-feudal territories and possessions, some for which were the possessions of dynasties which ruled over other countries and other areas of Europe. In 1786, shortly before the final suppression of the empire, within its borders were counted around 315 territories (kingdoms, grand duchies, duchies, principalities, etc.), along with 51 imperial cities and 1500 free cities. The Habsburg Emperor himself was more preoccupied with the multi-national state emerging from the intertwining of his possessions, than with the destinies of the empire as a whole. When, in 1778, Marie-Theresa of Austria invaded Bavaria, seeking a territorial expansion of her dynastic possessions, it became clear to what extent the two interests could be in a collision course.

The Pope, now without an exclusive dominion of Christianity, was reduced to the rank of a monarch, with whom one could make alliances or against whom one could fight. The age of religious wars ended with an historic compromise: *cuius regio, cuius religio*. The religious faith of an entire people would be determined by its king or prince. As had happened many centuries earlier, the conversion to Christendom of peoples was decided by the conversion of their chief.

A sovereign could certainly be tolerant towards his subjects of a different faith: he could give them a limited protection and allow them to settle in a certain region. The Protestants were welcomed in Transylvania, which belonged to the Catholic Habsburg Empire. But for most European states, one exclusive religious faith was to be the norm. Towards the end of the seventeenth century, an implacable persecution came down upon the many Protestants who still lived in Catholic France. Conversions were obtained by force, or bought with money. In 1685, a hard edict was enacted that meant to end the plurality of faiths, which were considered a blemish on the state. The Protestants would have to convert *en masse*. They were forbidden to emigrate. Nevertheless, 300,000 people escaped the grip of the state, finding asylum in Switzerland, Holland, and many little states of the German Empire.

The absolute monarch, who was identified with the state, could decide the denomination of his subjects with a decree. This opened the door to a ruthless control of religious cults by the state and its transformation into a new intolerant religion: the cult of the state.

The states—national and multi-national—were involved in a risky game of equilibrium, which intensified even more after 1648. An unwritten law of this game defined the powers, the protagonists of European politics, the actors who had the right to subsistence and the pursuit of their interests. In order to avoid that the satisfaction of one party did not harm another, many stop-gap solutions were developed, along with the creation of buffer zones, and many subtle regulatory mechanisms.

The developments in the arts of war and diplomacy made war the regulating mechanism *par excellence*. They produced a form of ritualization of conflict, which multiplied local conflicts avoiding (for the moment) more general conflagrations. Wars were seen as a way to obtain an exchange with advantageous concessions. The enemy was not attacked in order to destroy him, nor was there any intention of damaging civilian populations. Likewise the cultural relations between states were not interrupted by hostilities conducted by professional soldiers. War was rather a way to score points, and to change the equilibrium in the areas was considered of great interest. One could say that a contending party would declare war in order to arrive at the ensuing peace treaty in the most favorable position.

The game of reciprocal adjustments left considerable room for maneuvering. Along the possessions of the great power, there were vast spaces open for expansion. The peoples and individuals who lived there were not considered as having the right to decide their own destiny, to generate or conserve independent political subjects. The collapse of the European center allowed many contenders to control, directly or indirectly, a part of the German territories and principalities. Ever more frequently included in the game of conflicts and concessions were seaports, islands, and extremely vast extra-European territories: in India and North America, France and Britain fought distant wars which became an essential factor in maintaining equilibrium on European soil.

With the passing of years, vast regions of east-central Europe started being conceived as territories of conquest to be divided up.

Poland became the prey of the three bordering powers (Russia, Prussia, Austria) who, within two decades, suppressed its independence, divided its regions among themselves, and added a substantial number of Poles to their ethnic makeup.

Farther south, the Ottoman Empire was also in decline. It had reached its maximum extension at the end of the seventeenth century, with the second failed siege of Vienna. In a few years, the Habsburg counter-offensive made Austria the new master of the Balkans. Nevertheless, the Ottoman Empire resisted for a while: in 1739 the border stabilized along the Danube. Austria had re-conquered the kingdoms of Hungary and Croatia, the principality of Transylvania and all the regions the dynasty claimed as its own. In the second half of the eighteenth century the Russian Empire ended a journey which brought it possession of the plains of the Ukraine, the Crimean peninsula, and the coast of the Black Sea. In 1812 it tore from the Ottomans Bessarabia, a territory approximately the size of today's independent Republic of Moldavia, populated largely by Rumanians.

The Ottoman Empire had maintained vast possessions on European soil. But it had become the "sick man" of Europe.

# 6

## 1789/1815

### The "national contagion"

In the eighteenth century, states began to know the exact extent and configuration of their territories. In previous centuries, communities were often unaware to which state they belonged to, nor had they ever met representatives of the central power. Kings, princes, and emperors could only get an idea of the extent of their territories with exhaustive explorations of the interior. In the eighteenth century, absolute monarchs, now settled in very few locations, promoted a detailed process of cartography of their territories, which was quickly shared with the population.

A new interest was awakened in the nature and diversity of national characteristics. At a time when the biblical story of creation was being challenged as a source of authority to define the origin of the species, the story of the Tower of Babel was becoming less convincing as an authoritative explanation of the origins of nations. Perspectives derived from the new geological history were applied to the history of humanity. Climate and natural configuration of locales were at times given absolute power in the construction of human society. On the other hand, there were those who decisively defended the autonomy of society, culture, and human affairs.

For more than two years, from 1789 until the end of 1791, the French Revolution was above all an internal event. It spread throughout Europe only when Louis XVI sought assistance from the Austrian and Prussian dynasties. When, on the 20th of April 1792, the Constituent Assembly voted for war, he felt it to be an indispensable defensive necessity.

But the war quickly shifted from being defensive to being offensive. It led the French army to push far into central Europe, into Holland, Germany, Italy, into territories that were not ethnically French, and which had never belonged to the French state. An immediate goal was reaching a so-called "natural" border, which would crown the French eastward expansion and protect the conquests of the revolution: the Rhine. But the Rhine traversed territory which was ethnically German, on both shores.

French expansionism was a dramatic boost for those Germans who had hoped for the transformation of a fragmented and beaten Germany into a new and united state. Reacting to French pressure, the Germans also formulated an illusory perspective on so-called "natural" borders. According to opinions prevalent in Germany, these borders would have to be much further west: on the Moselle, for instance, which crossed French territory. From both sides, the germs were sown for a patriotism which could any minute degenerate into aggressive nationalism. And the conditions were created for a conflict which was to continue for more than a century, and which, combining with new conflicts in other areas of Europe, was to drag the entire continent into ruin.

In the short term, the French prevailed.

After a number of adventures, Napoleon took the last steps of the long journey which, in the centuries of the Modern Age, had weakened the authority of imperial and papal seats, in favor of the power of national states. He abolished the agonized simulation of the Holy Roman Empire. Earlier, he had placed on his own head, without any papal legitimation, the crown of a new multi-national empire, which had in the French national state its nucleus and its engine. The borders of this empire went from Hamburg to Rome, and resembled those of the empire of the Franks, a thousand years earlier. Napoleon tried to recreate a new center of Europe, based on a new power and a new secular belief. As in the medieval designs, the new order would have to be completed by "border marches:" a peripheral band that was integrated and homogenous with the central nucleus. To attract the aspirations of peoples frustrated by the previous order, the Kingdom of Italy was created, along with the Kingdom of Naples, the Republic of Helvetia, the Grand Duchy of Warsaw, a German Confederation of the Rhine.... The new empire seemed the natural conclusion to the crusade started by extremist revolutionaries right after the fateful year of 1789. "The territory which separates Paris from St. Petersburg will become Gallicized, municipalized, Jacobinized." But the reckless Russian campaign and the broadening of anti-French coalitions soon led to the collapse of the new Napoleonic order. Between 1789 and 1815, in France as in the European space that looked to Paris as it center, ideologies, ideas, political and geopolitical practices were outlined which in time would become the heritage of all Europe.

That all the areas of our continent belong to a state authority, that these state authorities are mutually exclusive, that a nation-state coincides intrinsically with a continuous and extended territory, that a nation-state has ethnic, historical, and geographic claims on a territory: today, these are all givens. Indeed, over the past century they have spread all over the world. Nevertheless, they are very recent assumptions. They asserted themselves precisely in this critical period from 1792 to 1814.

Before the revolution, at the Eastern margins of France, at the border of the Holy Roman Empire, there were fortresses and city-states tied by mutual accords both to the kingdom and the empire, that acted as buffer-zones. They were areas upon which sovereignties were superimposed. By spreading over pre-revolutionary borders, the French armies annexed all these areas. When, in 1814, France had to once more retreat and give up to the German Confederation (heir to the Holy Roman empire) many of its occupied territories, and buffer-zones were exchanged for clear borders.

It was not a restoration, but a revolution.

The new representation of borders and territories spread quickly in the imagination of all the peoples of Europe. In the journeys of emancipation, they claimed clear borders, declared "natural" and inviolable. The call to nature was hiding, as often happens, a mixture of cultural decisions, often unilateral and contingent.

In 1789-90, before the revolutionary army spread throughout Europe, decisive debates had taken place in the French Constituent Assembly regarding the definition of the form of the new state. One of the first and most important decisions was the abolition of the feudal regulations which had accumulated over a millennium. With them, a complex web of regions was abolished, each of which had its own local institutional forms and rights. The regional delegates themselves felt the importance of this development. The delegates of Brittany and Anjoux, asserted that they were no longer Bretons or Anjouins, but only French, *citizens of a single nation.*

Against the localism of earlier times, a solution was outlined that was exactly the opposite: the state would be divided into 81 equal departments, geometrically drawn in the form of squares. Some constituents revolted, arguing for history, tradition, geography, customs, and economics. In the end, there was a compromise. Every department—which had administrative and fiscal functions and provided for the election of deputies—would be designed, keeping pre-existing constraints in mind, and individuated by a name based on a local river or a mountain. In those same debates, the constituents voted to transform the 38,000 parishes into which France was divided, into autonomous communes, each with a mayor directly elected by the people. Both levels (communes and departments) were to have their own elected assemblies.

Along with the linguistic centralization of the previous centuries came political centralization. In 1800, Napoleon Bonaparte, immediately after the successful *coup d'état* , placed at the head of every department a prefect without the constraints of the elected assemblies, nominated by, and directly dependent on, the supreme state authorities. It was a solution imitated by many other states.

To the inextricable connection between state, nation, and territory, in post-revolutionary times another key idea was added: the fatherland. The revolutionaries, starting with the national anthem, filled this term with symbolism designed to signal a radical break with the past and transfer sovereignty from the monarch to the people. Fundamentally, the fatherland was understood as the totality of relations between individuals, defined after and due to the abolition of the feudal order. The fatherland consisted of citizens, those who had common goods and interests, and who contributed to building the new community, defined by rights and duties. The fatherland, on the other hand, was denied to aristocrats, and to those who refused, or fought, the new community.

The fatherland took over the nation.

The common imaginary created by the absolute monarchs of the preceding centuries was inverted. The revolutionaries were successful, but they left ambiguities and unresolved problems. They were successful because many French already had a strongly defined national identity. They transferred their loyalty to a new social body, and intensified it: when war broke out, they were ready to take up arms. Nevertheless, the construction of the nation was on the one hand incomplete, and on the other *too* complete. It had been accompanied by latent and unresolved tensions with nations or subject regions, with nations that could have emerged and did not, with regional identities that looked to the past, or outside national borders. Not accidentally, the aristocrats, those without a fatherland, found their greatest following where the construction of the common identity had been weakest and most authoritarian: in rural regions, where the local came before the national, and border regions, where ties with other nations were strongest.

The revolutionaries reacted harshly. Barère asserted that superstition spoke Breton, hatred for the republic spoke German, the counter-revolution spoke Italian, and concluded that a free people should speak the same language. Starting in 1794, regional languages were repressed. Steps were also taken to ensure that all citizens develop a mastery of French.

The roads taken by the revolutionary were ambivalent.

On the one hand, the primacy of the fatherland over the nation led to the development of a concept of citizenship as distinct as possible from genealogies or races, founded in principle on free choice and voluntary membership, and indifferent towards the particulars of history and individual and collective roots. It is precisely because of this concept that in the nineteenth and early-twentieth centuries France revealed itself as the most hospitable nation for immigration, integrating into its society new citizens originating throughout Europe, and then from non-European continents. To this day, around a quarter of all French citizens has at least one second-generation ancestor of foreign origin. This strategy would go into crisis the moment that extra-European immigrants began to exceed those of European origin: for many groups, renouncing their own peculiarities and their own roots would not be at all easy.

On the other hand, as with the case of territorial unities, the post-revolutionary idea of the nation-state came perilously close to the primacy of theory over history, of rationality defined in a meeting room over concrete reality, of the effacing of history over a multiplicity of histories, of homogenization over diversity.... Was it necessary for a common fatherland to impose only one nation and only one language? Was it necessary for it to impose an elimination of individual histories and roots? Was it inevitable that the indifference to the particularity of histories and roots should be interpreted as oblivion and obscuring of these histories and roots? If the events prior to 1648 imposed on many European states one faith at the expense of experimentation with a plurality of faiths, the events after 1789 imposed on many European states a single nationality, at the expense of experimentation with multiple nationalities.

The message of the revolutionaries, "one fatherland, one nation," was also: "to every nation, its fatherland." This was how the message was understood not only in Germany and Italy, but also in distant Serbia, Greece, and Rumania.

But what would happen if the nation were not yet accompanied by a state? And where the dominant states had not yet forged new nations, but had, in fact, attempted to cover up ancient nations? And where the identity of many individuals and collectivities was uncertain, oscillating, contested? And where multi-nationality and multiple faiths were a fact of everyday life?

After 1815, Europe was neatly divided into three areas.

In the first area, the West and Scandinavia, were nation-states with identities that had been consolidated over centuries: France, Spain, Portugal, England, Denmark, Sweden. After 1648, Switzerland and the Low Countries joined them.

In the second area, to the East of the first, the heritage of the vanquished Holy Roman Empire left a space for around fifty small kingdoms, grand duchies, duchies, principalities, and city-states. Two nations, Germany and Italy, were in search of their respective states.

Even further East, the relation between states and nations was exactly the opposite. Many ethnicities were part of only four multi-national entities: the Ottoman Empire, the Russian Empire, the Kingdom of Prussia (which, having annexed the lands of eastern Poland, now included a Slavic population), and the Austrian Empire. The latter had been created by the union of all the Habsburg territories when Napoleon abolished the Holy Roman Empire. The dynasty's center of gravity had thus moved definitively Eastward, towards the Danube and the Balkans.

This Europe, divided by geographic areas, was the theater of a real "contagion" of the nation-state, a contagion which moved from the west to the east. With the diffusion of the prestige and the ideals of revolutionary France, the aspirations to make ethnic unity coincide with political unity were generalized throughout Europe.

The contagion of the nation-state has defined the entire era from 1815 to the present.

And it is an ambivalent contagion, in terms of the effects it produced, because it has allowed great and irreversible conquests for the collectivity and for the European people, but it has also sown the seeds for the worst catastrophes. The national movements of the various peoples have walked a razor's edge, between the legitimate affirmation of their rights and the tendency to prevaricate over other nationalities which history, geography, and culture have placed on collision course.

History from 1815 to 1993 has shown sufficiently how the relationships between state, nation, and ethnicity are different, and just as problematic, in every corner of Europe.

# 7

## From the Atlantic to the North Sea

### Ancient nations, emerging regions

Originating in apparently similar assumptions, the "contagion" of nation-states had very different outcomes in the three bands into which Europe in 1815 was already divided.

Western Europe has been devastated by the Franco-German conflicts of 1870, 1914, and 1939 (the last two were episodes of great European and World Wars that started elsewhere). But as a whole, it has enjoyed a surprising stability in its prevailing order considering the continuous changes of the previous centuries. In this part of Europe, the changes in borders were really minimal. In fact, some of these borders are older than Europe: the border between Spain and France goes back to 1659; between Spain and Portugal to 1640 (and ultimately to even earlier centuries). This stability of the prevailing order is even more noticeable if we think of the fact that in 1945, after a century of bitter warfare, the border and possession of Alsace-Lorraine returned to the status quo ante of 1815.

It is therefore not by chance, that the process of "de-dramatization" of borders, one of the most interesting contributions of the European Community, should have originated in precisely this part of Europe.

New states have also been created in this part of Europe: Belgium, Luxembourg, Norway, Iceland, and Ireland.

Belgium and Ireland to this day present open questions, for reasons that are in some way opposites: because of a too weak identity in one case, and because of an extremely rooted one in the other.

In both cases, independence has been defined on the basis of religion, not language. In 1830, Belgium was constituted through the separation of the southern regions of the Kingdom of Holland (largely Catholic) from the rest of the country (both Catholic and Protestant). The Republic of Ireland was constituted after the World War I, through the separation of the southern regions of the island (largely Catholic) from the northern regions (Ulster, a mix of Catholics and Protestants). The latter remained a part of the United Kingdom.

No linguistic border separated Belgium and Holland. On the contrary, Belgium was and is divided by a clear internal linguistic border, which is also perceived as an ethnic-national border, separating the Flemish (Dutch speakers) from the Walloons (French speakers). Two other factors have complicated the Belgian national mosaic: the annexation, at the end of World War I, of German speaking border areas; and the peculiar story of the city of Brussels, which, situated in the Flemish region, has become a bilingual city with a French majority. These stratifications, coupled with a series of economic and cultural divergences, have ensured that there should not emerge a national identity separate from the ethno-linguistic identities. They have ensured, on the other hand, that they should continue to pose a menace to the state's identity.

The territory of today's Republic of Ireland, on the other hand, was and is bilingual: Gaelic is spoken along with English. In Ireland the linguistic borders have never been felt as ethnic or national borders. Rather, a nation has progressively changed language while still continuing to feel like a single nation. In the centuries of English domination, there was a shift from the situation in 1600 (when Gaelic was the majority language) to the situation in 1800 (when English had became the language of the upper class), to the situation in the first few years of the twentieth century (when fewer than 20% of the population spoke Gaelic).

Today, English is the language used by the entire population. Irish Gaelic, on the other hand, is the daily language of a restricted number of people living in the so-called *Gaeltacht*, in the extreme west of the island. But it is the island's official language next to English. In fact it is the "first" language. It is of considerable importance in the educational system, to the point that almost a third of the Irish today claim to know the language. More generally, Gaelic is considered an important part of Ireland's historical identity, a heritage from the centuries in which Celtic Christianity conserved and spread the memories of the classical world. In Ireland, the historical identity (of which linguistic identity is only a part) has added itself to a strong religious identity, to generate a sense of national identity that has resisted, for centuries, the leveling pressures of English domination.

The case of Ireland is the case of a nation that has not only stayed in existence, but is also capable of becoming the nucleus of a new nation-state, after centuries of annexation to the state of the British crown. This experience can be compared with the surprising resistance of the national identities of the Welsh and the Scots, who have also, for years, been annexed to the United Kingdom. In Scotland and Wales there are also two Celtic languages comparable to Irish (and today Welsh is more common as a first language than Irish). But the feeling of belonging to a separate nationality goes much beyond the restricted Celtic language communities: it involves many individuals who have known English to be the only language for centuries, and it has spread throughout the entire territory. It is a feeling of common nationality based on historical rather than linguistic roots.

The behavior of the Welsh and the Scots is to a certain extent similar to that of the English themselves. The English also maintain their sense of historical-regional identity (*English*) separate from the state community to which they belong (*British*). *English* and *British* are two terms that accompany each other and are used interchangeably in discussions, depending on circumstance and context. We can then sum up the question by stating that in the United Kingdom of Great Britain, there emerges a system of nationality on two levels: English, Welsh, Scots, at a more local level; British at a more general level. The linguistic aspect of this system is now marginal.

On the continent, many ethnicities that were similarly integrated into the nation-states of France and Spain during their territorial unification have rediscovered their identity: Basques, Catalans, Corsicans, Bretons. In their relations with the central powers, depending on contexts, individuals, collectivities, and public opinion, they ask for autonomy, recognition of their national sovereignty, or, in the most extreme cases, secession from the states they are part of. Unlike the case of the British Isles, for the ethnic minorities of France and Spain linguistic identity is fundamental in defining national identity: the preservation of their own language has been one of the crucial factors in their rediscovery of roots.

Both in France and in Spain, there is a polarization in the structure of the ethno-linguistic territory. A vast central body (centering around the capital and the regions that were the aggregating nucleus of the nation-states) is linguistically homogeneous, a testimony to the relative antiquity of these areas' processes of unification. A peripheral zone opposes this central body, populated by individuals of ethnic minorities, who belong to nationalities that do not have their own state, or to nationalities that are the majority in bordering states.

Let us follow the maritime and terrestrial borders of the "Hexagon," the French state. Flemish, or, if we prefer, Netherlandish (a term that includes in one language both Dutch and Flemish) dialects are spoken in the littoral area on the border with Belgium. Alsace and Lorraine are regions where German dialects prevail. Corsicans speak an archaic Tuscan dialect. The entire area of the Pyrenees adjacent to the borders with Spain, from Rossillon to the Bay of Biscay, is home to large Basque and Catalan communities, which have the central nucleus of their population in Spanish territory. On the Atlantic, in the western part of Brittany, a Celtic idiom, originating in the British Isles, is still spoken, due to migration in the High Middle Ages.

The situation of the southern regions (*Midi*), Provençe, and Alpine Arch is quite particular. With time, the original diversification of the Neo-latin dialects became stratified into two languages, the *langue d'oïl* (western) and the *langue d'oc*, (southern). In an area of transitional languages, with their own characteristics they were eventually defined by linguists as an autonomous language: Franco-Provençal. In the Middle Ages, the *langue d'oïl* and the *langue d'oc* both enjoyed great literary prestige. But the choice of the new nation-state led to the ascent of the first (which was now French *tout court*) to the role of the great language of culture. It confined the second (Occitanian or Provençal) to the sphere of private communication. As a consequence, today, all western speakers are bilingual, using French in a large part of their public life. If, therefore, a significant part of French society originates in regions where Occitanian is spoken, the number of those who consider themselves as belonging to the Occitanian nationality, as an integral part of their identity, is much smaller. Estimates are difficult: at least ten million in the first case, two million in the second.

All the regions we have discussed have slowly been reached by the expansion and centralization of the French state. The *Midi* and Provençe, assimilated at the end of the Middle Ages, have, for centuries, retained their own laws and autonomous statutes. Brittany was one of the last regional identities to give in to the new power of the sovereign. The possession of Rossillon dates back to 1659, Corsica to 1768, and some of the regions of the Alpine Arch (Savoy) to 1860. The annexation of Alsace and Lorraine started only in 1648, and was completed with the French revolution, apart from the two times it was revoked (1871 and 1940), after which it was twice regained (1919, 1945).

In Spain, the emergence of a national center at the end of the Middle Ages also simplified the ethno-linguistic situation. Castilian became the language of culture, absorbing a vast number of Asturian, Leonese, and Aragonian dialects, which had previously been more diversified. As the

*Reconquista* proceeded all the southern regions were conquered by Castilian. But in the North, peculiar ethno-linguistic identities remained. In the northwestern corner of Spain, Galician is spoken, considered by many to be transitional between Castilian and Portuguese, and by others a variation *tout court* on Portuguese. In the northeast, from the French border to Valencia, Catalan (another neo-Latin language clearly differentiated from Castillian and closer to Occitanian) is spoken. The Basques, with their ancient, non-Indo-European language populate the western Pyrenees and the regions adjacent to the Bay of Biscay. In Spain, the minority nationalities are a substantial part of the population, occupy compact territories, have a strong awareness of their historical roots, and, moreover, are generally located in areas with considerable economic and industrial development.

In the last two centuries, in France as in Spain, latent ethnic conflicts have been fostered both by the centralizing structure of the states and the simplistic language politics. In both cases these have attempted to transform, respectively, French and Spanish from *élite* literary languages to national languages accessible to all citizens. In this way they have excluded from their school systems the study of, and reference to, other internal languages and dialects of the national language (which are often confused in an indistinct category). In the age of positivism, the local language, site of the private, of emotion, of memory, inherent in the roots of a country's past, is often rhetorically opposed to the official language, intended for public, rational, institutional communication. As a reaction, cultural streams of a more romantic bent often favor the rediscovery of minority languages and cultures.

In the years between 1931 and 1933, Spain began the stipulation of a new national pact which would liberate it from the constraints of this policy. The civil war turned the situation upside down. Catalan became interwoven with a very clear Anti-Franco choice. Consequently, in Catalonia, the Franco regime not only exercised repression at the social and political level, but it also enforced a homogenization of language and culture.

Today, France and Spain are rethinking the history of the last two centuries: the latent and overt ethnic tensions; the unintended political effects of centralization; and, above all, of the homogenization of language and culture.

In France, nevertheless, the rediscovery and re-appraisal of what are known as the "regional languages" is largely in the hands of individuals and individual groups. The state, for its part, remains absent and continues the policy begun in 1539: French is the only public language. But in 1951, the Deixonne Law smashed a dogma: Public schools could now organize electives in "regional languages."

On the level of territorial organization, the French state remains largely centralized. In 1982, France was divided into 22 regions, each with its own elected assemblies and executive. But the regions have no control over the traditional territorial units (departments and municipalities) and have limited competencies. Furthermore, the identities of the new regions themselves are weak and unpopular: they are agglomerations of departments, rather than the revivification of ancient historical entities. There is also no tie between their identities and the ethno-linguistic identities which, as we have seen, are so abundant in France. There is one exception: Corsica, where ethnic and geographic borders coincide. Corsica is the only autonomous region in the French system, with greater powers and, above all, its own cultural institutions. Its assembly has recognized the existence of the Corsican people as a historical and cultural community.

In post-Franco Spain, the policy is different. The constitution of 1978 has, in part, recognized the multi-national nature of the state, and speaks of the nationalities, people, and languages of Spain. Since then, Spain has tightly interwoven the ethnic and regional question. It has responded to the demands for self-government expressed by the minority nationalities, through a policy of regionalization throughout the entire state.

Spanish territory has been divided into 17 autonomous communities, each enjoying different degrees of competence and self-government. At times this can involve fiscal competencies. In other cases, it does not even extend to education. Furthermore, it is up to the autonomous communities which official language (if any) their territory is to add to Spanish.

Among these communities, some have a mostly linguistic identity (Catalonia, the Basque provinces, Galicia); others have a largely geographic identity (the Balearic and Canary Islands); others have a largely historical identity (Andalusia); and others have an identity that is somewhere between the ethno-linguistic and the historical (Aragon and Valencia, Catalan is spoken by a part of the population, but in smaller number than in Catalonia). Navarra, in particular, has a strong historical identity, tied to memories of the old medieval kingdom, and a clashing ethno-linguistic identity: 10% of the population speaks Basque, and often calls for reintegration into the Basque Provinces, while the majority of Castilian speakers consider Basque foreign to its regional identity.

In any case, the new regional identities are becoming an integrating part of the national identity of Spanish citizens, which somehow is a system configured along two levels.

The reform has been quite successful, particularly in the communities with Spanish (Castilian) language and culture often pushed to rediscover roots and particular memories of the past. On the other hand, the Catalan question and the Basque question are still open. In 1989 and 1990, the parliaments of the autonomous communities of Catalonia and the Basque Province voted for declarations which reclaimed their respective rights of national self-determination and which submit to their jurisdiction the most opportune ways in which to exercise this right. At this time, the Catalans and Basques seem divided: between those who agree to take part in the larger community of the Spanish state, and those who prefer the creation of a national state. For the Catalan community, as for the Basque community, the possibility is open that they might become nations constituting a Spanish state re-defining itself from mono-national to multi-national. In the opposite case, there is the difficult prospect of defining new states exposed to all the risks of mono-nationalities in regions which have been multi-national for centuries.

# 8

## Germany

### From nation to state, from state to regions

Eighteenth-century Germans (still nominally integrated in the German Empire, but in reality divided into innumerable territories), had already developed a strong sense of belonging to a common nation, based on language, folkways, and customs. If and when this nation was to become a state was a question highly debated among cultivated persons and the upwardly mobile, whereas in Paris there was a reunion of the states general.

In 1815, after the tornado that was Napoleon, the war of liberation against the French reinforced the objective of national unification. This objective clashed both with the aspirations of individual rulers (who sought a return to a pre-1792 order), and with the strategic vision of the great powers (who viewed Central Europe as a passive buffer in struggles over equilibrium). Although public opinion agreed on the objective of unification, there was no agreement on the extent and manner of unification.

Actually, the decisions of 1815 simplified the German world's territorial panorama. The intricate mosaic of small states, imperial cities, and free castles, was redistributed into 39 entities made up of territorial states and free cities. The new entities were of very different dimensions and institutional forms, interwoven and wedged together. They ranged from Austrian regions of the Habsburg Empire (including the Tyrol, Carniola, Bohemia and Moravia) to the vast Kingdom of Prussia; from the four kingdoms (which could be defined as regional) of Bavaria, Württemberg, Saxony and Hanover, to the electoral principality of Hesse and the four city-states of Hamburg, Bremen, Lübeck and Frankfurt. The picture was completed by 7 grand duchies (Baden, Hesse-Darmstadt, Luxembourg, Mecklenburg-Schwerin, Oldenburg, Saxony-Weimar), 7 duchies (Braunschweig, Holstein, Lauenburg, Nassau, Saxony-Altenburg, Saxony-Coburg-Gotha, Saxony-Meiningen) and 14 principalities, which in many regions pulverized the German territory.

The Congress of Vienna decided to reconstruct the two-level system of authority that had characterized Europe for a thousand years. Along with the individual states there would also be a German confederation, with a parliament, made up of delegates from the various governments. But the new structure was weakened not only by institutional differences and the differences in the demographic and economic weight of the various states, but also by recurring conflicts between Austria and Prussia, rivals for a leadership role in the new confederation.

There were more complications.

A part of the possessions of the royal houses of Austria and Prussia had, in fact, never belonged to the now-defunct empire, and was, therefore, not admitted into the territory of the confederation. For Prussia, it was Prussia itself and its recently annexed Polish territories. For Austria, it was Hungary, Croatia, Galicia, and Bukovina. Austria and Prussia had been multi-national states that included ethnicities other than Germans. At the same time, the German confederation did not exhaust the regions populated by Germans. Germans were in the majority in many Swiss cantons, a considerable minority throughout East-Central Europe: even in regions such as the Baltic countries and the Volga, which belonged to the Russian Empire.

In the end, the German confederation turned out to be the last heir of a medieval international law, antecedent to the system of exclusive borders between states, which by now had become generally applicable. The Habsburg Empire and the Kingdom of Prussia were not the only ones to have one foot inside and one foot outside as far as the confederation went. There were other countries in analogous situations: Denmark, with the duchy of Holstein; Holland, with the grand duchy of Luxembourg; and England itself, united with Hanover.

Some very delicate questions were asked in this complicated scenario.

Should German unity occur top-down, by the extension and clustering around one of the dominant powers (Prussia or Austria), or bottom-up, through federal constraints which respected the identity and rights of the members of the confederation? Was the space of the emerging Germany supposed to include only the territories of the present confederation, or should it broaden to include the territories of Prussia and Austrian? Would there have to be an organizing framework built around an intermediate configuration, such as the entire Kingdom of Prussia and part of the regions of the Austrian Empire? Or should Austria be excluded altogether?

The extremely varied ethnic composition of the Habsburg Empire made its inclusion in the German state, in its entirety, very problematic. In Prussia, in the internal and external parts of the confederation, with the German majority there was only the strong Polish ethnic group (1.5 million). In the Habsburg Empire of 1849, 6,400,000 Germans were accompanied by 14,820,000 Slavs, 5,305,000 Magyars, 4,584,000 Italians, and also Rumanians, Jews, Gypsies, Greeks, Albanians, and Armenians. Just looking at the figures for the Austrian territories belonging to the German confederation, the 5,340,000 Germans which populated them were accompanied by a Slav group of almost equal size (5,235,000), with 200,000 in Trieste and the Tyrol. The question arose whether, only the part of Austria where the German element was in the majority should be included, so as not to water down the ethnic character of Germany. But how could it be expected that Austria renounce territories and peoples that had been so important to its history? These kinds of questions contributed to weakening the Habsburg position, to Prussia's advantage.

In 1848, possibilities were enunciated and opinions clashed. On the 18th of May, the Paulskirche in Frankfurt saw the first sitting of 580 deputies of a German national assembly. It was elected by the citizens of the states of the confederation with the mandate to "finalize the German constitutional duty, placing itself between the government and the people." In preceding months, popular uprisings, changes at high levels of state, loyalties to princes and sovereigns (made with conviction or opportunism), made national unification into a concrete objective. The work lasted thirteen months, alternating hope and disappointment.

The assembly was stuck on two crucial questions. The first was: what should the exact borders of Germany be? Despite noble objections, it was clear that, for areas with mixed populations (Prussia's Polish possessions or Austria's Italian possessions), the deputies were not concerned with subtleties: they were largely to be included in the new state, with few guarantees for the rights of non-Germans. The arguments were often dismissive and disconcerting. They spoke of "victors" and the "rights of possession," and considered "German dominion over the Slavs" a "natural and historical fact." German hostility to the Slavs was returned. Bohemian Czechs and Slovenians in Carniola announced that they would secede if the Habsburg dominions were annexed by Germany.

The second question was more burning: with Austria (the *Grossdeutsch* solution) or without Austria (the *Kleindeutsch* solution)? The assembly's proposal, expressed in quite intricate and obscure terms, invited Austria to seek an institutional formula that divided German from non-German territories. This was clearly unacceptable for the Austrians, who, in fact, communicated their rejection. In the end, the Assembly resolved to exclude Austria, fully accepting the *"Kleindeutsch"* position. Immediately afterward, it proposed the election of Frederick Wilhelm IV, King of Prussia. The disenchantment was scorching. The king, emboldened by the support of the European powers explained how the winds had changed, and how sovereigns once more held the upper hand. To have the crown, offered by the Assembly and not by the princes of the states, would be an intolerable "iron collar of servitude." The end was inglorious. The intervention of the reinvigorated Prussian and Austrian armies led to the end of the assemblies, and with that, all hope for a unification from below. The only choice that remained was unification from above.

The competition between Prussia and Austria continued. In the end, an apparently marginal disagreement (differences regarding the juridical status of the northernmost territory of the confederation, the duchy of Holstein) led to the minor German states finally taking a position in alliance with one of the two rivals. In 1866 Prussia dealt Austria a serious defeat, which led the Habsburg emperor to direct his attention elsewhere. Not by chance, the following year saw the metamorphosis of the Austrian Empire into the Austro-Hungarian Empire. As the last remaining great power of Germany, Prussia took pains to strengthen its hegemony in the Western part of the confederation, seeking to obtain as continuous a territory as possible between the Rhine and Baltic Seas, and in the process annexing some illustrious states: the Kingdom of Hanover and the city-state of Frankfurt. It exercised more distanced hegemony on the southern states, pushing them to adhere to a new customs confederation (*zollverein*), which had its own parliament.

The final and decisive step was made only a little later, between 1870 and 1871. A new success in war for Prussia and its allies, against France, gave them regions of great strategic importance: Alsace and Lorraine. In the euphoria of victory, Wilhelm I, King of Prussia, was crowned Emperor of the Second Reich.

Had the Germans found the nation-state they so longed for?

The *"Kleindeutsch"* solution, which excluded Austria, was chosen more because of pressing events than careful deliberation. In any case, outside of the new empire were many millions of citizens sharing a German culture and the German language who now found themselves in Habsburg territory. Moreover, the empire (*Reich*) was still constituted of more than twenty states (*Länder*), each with its own sovereign and its own assemblies. These states were added to the central authorities and institutions, with possible conflicts of power and competencies. We remember that Bismarck suffered a stinging defeat when he attempted to introduce a tobacco monopoly in the *Reich*; and we remember, above all, that the various states did not stop running their own railways until 1918.

Furthermore, the territorial structure itself was very unbalanced. In the German confederacy (1857), Prussia covered only 29.6% of the territory and 30.5% of the population. But the second empire had been generated by a further expansion of Prussia, by the integration of the ancient Prussian territories to the first empire, and, on the other hand, by the expulsion of the Austrian territories. In the new system (1890), Prussia covered 64.5% of the entire surface, and had 60.6% of the population. Next to her, there were not only some medium-sized regional states, (Bavaria, Württemberg, Saxony), but also many of the ancient minor principalities. Paradoxically, the structure was at the same time distant and close to the model of the French centralized state. It was distant, because if the French model was knowingly based on a rupture with all history before 1789, the German territorial model kept the memory of many accidents and irrationalities of history. It was close, because more than half the population was still subjected to Prussian administration, which at least in the Western part extended from the western margins to the eastern margins of the new empire.

After the defeat of the First World War, the identity problems of the German nation-state were inherited by the new republic. In 1919, the constituents of Weimar cared little about the internal structure of the state, caught up as they were in the more pressing dilemma of whether or not to accept the peace clauses of the Treaty of Versailles, which to many sounded like an unjust punishment. The new federal constitution attempted to improve the balance between central authority and the authority of the individual states. But even though there was no longer an Emperor or a King of Prussia, nor princes in the other states, the imbalances among the individual states remained. The internal structure, made up of a large Prussia surrounded by many historical curiosities, was transferred virtually unchanged into the new republic: only Thuringia swallowed a number of ancient principalities. As the data below show, in 1924 the structure remained unbalanced:

| Länder (States) | Area (Km²) | Population |
|---|---|---|
| Prussia | 294,555 | 36,690,549 |
| Bavaria | 76,421 | 7,140,333 |
| Württemberg | 19,507 | 2,518,773 |
| Baden | 15,070 | 2,208,503 |
| Saxony | 14,993 | 4,663,298 |
| Mecklenburg-Schwerin | 13,127 | 657,330 |
| Thuringia | 11,763 | 1,508,025 |
| Hesse-Darmstadt | 7,688 | 1,290,988 |
| Oldenburg | 6,429 | 517,765 |
| Braunschweig | 3,627 | 480,599 |
| Mecklenberg-Strelitz | 2,930 | 106,394 |
| Anhalt | 2,299 | 331,253 |
| Lippe-Detmold | 1,215 | 154,318 |
| Waldeck | 1,055 | 55,999 |
| Hamburg | 415 | 1,050,359 |
| Schaumberg-Lippe | 340 | 46,357 |
| Lübeck | 298 | 120,658 |
| Bremen | 256 | 311,266 |
| Total | 472,034 | 59,852,682 |

Prussia alone, therefore, corresponded to 62.4% of the surface and 61.3% of the republic's population. If we add Bavaria, the only other state which managed to retain a strong identity, we see that the two states together cover 78.6% of the surface and 73.2% of the population.

But more than anything it was the relation between Germany and the bordering states which threatened German democracy and peace in Europe. In reality, the new borders established by the treaty of Versailles had led to a diminution, but not a mutilation, of the German state. Many of the eastern regions Germany had to give up were populated mainly by Poles, an awkward legacy of eighteenth-century divisions. And already in 1916, the Kaiser had solemnly announced, in a joint declaration with the Habsburg emperor, that at the end of the war he would contribute to the re-establishment of Polish independence, giving up a part of his territory.

It was rather the considerable war reparations and the military arrangements which caused a scandal, and were perceived as limitations on national sovereignty. Viewing these clauses unfavorably, German public opinion crystallized around ethnic divisions, which were certainly not lacking. Certain territories that had been given to Poland contained German minorities; eastern Prussia had been cut of from the main body of the state, to give Poland an outlet at sea; Danzig, a city with a German majority, had been elected a free state, under the aegis of the League of Nations; Memel, another German port on the Baltic had been ceded to Lithuania....

Paradoxically, the most explosive question was the uncertain destiny of the communities and territories that were German-speaking and of German culture in the former Austria-Hungary. If the did not belong to the second empire *before* 1918. These communities and territories were at least united in a parallel empire, in which Germans constituted the core of the ruling class. Now, on the contrary, the peace treaties had dispersed them in many states, and in every one of those they found themselves in different conditions. In some states (Hungary, Yugoslavia, Rumania), Germans were minorities and scattered throughout the territory. In Austria, on the other hand, they were an absolute majority, and populated the entire territory. In Czechoslovakia, they made up an important part of the population, but above all they were confined to a compact band at the borders of Austria and Germany, where they were often an absolute majority.

Both in Austria and Czechoslovakia, the German identity crisis was felt very strongly. In the first case, the heirs of an extensive territory and a multinational past had to reinvent themselves in a small territory and a mononational present. In the second case, a dominant group had been turned into a minority. In 1919, the uncertain identity of Austria and Czechoslovakia forced a rethinking of the German question, not only for Germany, but also for the winners and for Europe as a whole. Instead, the winners decided that those most immediately concerned would not be consulted. For Austria, the possibility of a reunification with Germany was excluded. And Czechoslovakia inherited without revision the ancient kingdom of Bohemia.

The insane Nazi adventure took its lead from the internal and external disturbances in the German nation, amplified them, and turned the whole continent upside down. Adolf Hitler made use of the desire for revenge, which brought together Germans of the most disparate geographical origins, political opinions, and social classes. He replied to the injustices Germans felt they had suffered with ever greater violence and transgression, with ever greater inhumanity. In the space of a few years, no individual, no collectivity, no people in the region was able to freely decide on its destiny. Hitler and the Nazis fed the demon of an aggressive and totalitarian nationalism,

which continued to feed itself with ever more outrageous demands. The
Nazis interpreted the German claims in the most extensive and unilateral
way possible. The third Reich would have to include not only the areas with
a German majority, but also those areas with consistent German minorities,
the areas which in some previous century had belonged to the sphere of influence of the German peoples or state, the areas which were simply needed
for economic expansion....

   In a few years, the Nazi expansion took on an impressive rhythm, and involved equally impressive dimensions:

   In 1919, the Treaty of Versailles defined a German territory with a surface of 468,620
Km$^2$. In 1939, the inhabitants of this territory were 68,474,100.

   In March of 1935, Germany took back the little region of the Saar, which the Treaty
of Versailles had for fifteen years put under the auspices of the League of Nations.

   In March of 1938, Austria was annexed.

   In September of 1938, the inauspicious accords of Monaco allowed Germany to
annex the Czechoslovak region of the Sudetenland, with a German ethnic majority.

   In March of 1939, what was left of Bohemia and Moravia, with a Czech majority,
became subject to the Reich, under the particular formula of a Protectorate.

   In the same month, Germany launched an ultimatum to Lithuania, in order to take
back Memel (Klaipeda), which had been annexed by Lithuania in 1923.

   Danzig, the contested city which became the pretext for the invasion of Poland, was
annexed the very same day hostilities broke out: the 1st of September 1939, the date the
Second World War began.

   In three weeks, Germany had reached its objectives in Poland. On September 22
1939, a part of the oppressed state in which there were nuclei of German population, was
annexed directly to the Reich.

   Another sector of Poland was subjected to the Reich, this time with a Governor
General, similar to the Protectorate of Bohemia-Moravia.

   As soon as Belgium was invaded (May 1940), Germany took back the border lands,
which had a German majority and had been given up following the Treaty of Versailles.

   Luxembourg was also invaded and subjected to a German civil administration.

   In August of 1940, after the collapse of France, Alsace and Lorraine were annexed
again.

   After the invasion and dismemberment of Yugoslavia (April 1941), the northern
regions of Slovenia, in close proximity to the ancient borders of the Reich, were annexed.

When, on the 22nd of June 1941, the Nazi army attacked the Soviet Union, the German state as a whole (the *Grossdeutsches Reich*) covered a territory of 852,358 Km², with a population of more than 110 million, many of Slavic origin.

The catastrophe of 1945 exacerbated, if that is possible, the problem of the identity of the German nation-state and its foreign borders. The winners of the Second World War gave Poland the eastern regions of Germany (Prussia, Pomerania, Silesia), in which the German ethnic element was nevertheless predominant. From then on, in a few years, the very heart of the German population in Central Europe found itself divided not just in two, but in three states with the birth of the DDR, along with the hybrid entity that Berlin, the city under siege, became during the Cold War.

Nevertheless, the catastrophe created the foundations for a rethinking of the equally crucial question of the internal structure of the German state.

In July of 1945, the three great winners of the Second World War, the United States, the Soviet Union, and Great Britain, came together in Potsdam to make a series of decisions which were to mark the future of Europe for decades to come. The Soviet decision to transfer to Poland many eastern parts of Germany was taken as a given. It was decided that the remaining territory should be divided in four occupation areas (including France in the process), with the prospect of having them converge, sooner or later, into a new German state. The four zones were immediately subjected to a radical administrative reform. Every one of them was subdivided into new regional units, which combined the territories of the ancient states, enlarging and extending some, abolishing others, and subdividing in smaller parts the compact ancient territory of Prussia. The most amazing result was the abolition of the entity and the name "Prussia" itself. At that moment, the intuition of Wilhelm on becoming Emperor of Germany in 1871, which led him to say "Today we have buried the old Prussia," was finally accomplished.

The new administrative structure was incorporated into the Basic Law of the German Federal Republic (BRD), which was born the 23rd of May 1949 from the progressive fusion of the three American, English, and French occupation zones. With small changes, in the 1950's it was stabilized into a structure of 10 states (*Länder*), which to this day characterizes the western part of the reunited Germany. In the German Democratic Republic (DDR)— which arose out of the evolution and separation of the Soviet occupation zone in the first years of the cold war—the structure which had originally been put into position, with 5 Länder, was replaced in 1952 by a division into 15 small districts, which was more functional for a heavily planned and controlled economy.

In 1990, one of the most important decisions of the transitional assembly, which was to vote for the self-dissolution of the DDR and its inclusion in the German Federal Republic, was precisely the restoration of the 5 ancient Länder. These 5 Länder, along with the 10 Länder of the Western Regions, and the entire city of Berlin (which today has become a Land in its own right), make up the structure of 16 Länder, which characterizes the German state after the unification of the 3rd of October 1990. The differences from the Weimar arrangement are clear:

| Länder (States) | Area (Km$^2$) | Population (1990) |
|---|---|---|
| Bavaria | 70,554 | 11,448,823 |
| Lower Saxony | 47,351 | 7,387,245 |
| Baden-Württemberg | 35,752 | 9,882,027 |
| West Rheinland-Westfalia | 34,070 | 17,349,651 |
| Brandenburg | 29,056 | 2,578,312 |
| Mecklenburg-Pomerania | 23,559 | 1,923,959 |
| Hesse | 21,114 | 5,763,310 |
| Saxony-Anhalt | 20,607 | 2,873,957 |
| Rheinland-Palatinate | 19,849 | 3,763,510 |
| Saxony | 18,341 | 4,764,301 |
| Thuringia | 16,252 | 2,611,319 |
| Saarland | 2,570 | 1,072,963 |
| Berlin | 889 | 3,433,695 |
| Hamburg | 755 | 1,652,363 |
| Bremen | 404 | 681,665 |
| Total | 356,854 | 79,753,227 |

The new states are much more balanced in terms of surface, population, and economic weight. The largest state (Bavaria, whose surface totals 19.8% of the total surface of the Republic) is not even the most populated. The most populated state is Western Rheinland-Westfalia, with a population which amounts to 21.8% of the total population. The percentage of the surface area of the two largest Länder (Bavaria and Lower Saxony) goes up to 33% of the total surface, while the proportion of inhabitants of the two most highly populated Länder (Western-Rheinland-Westfalia and Bavaria) is at

36.1% of the total number of inhabitants. Figures which in any case are very different from those of the Weimar Republic.

The creation of balanced states has naturally not led to their homogenization. Less than ever has it imposed land area as a rigid normative criterion. Bremen and Hamburg have in fact found their ancient institutional form of city-state reconfirmed in the new German arrangement.

Compared to the arrangements of 1815, 1871, and 1919, some Länder of today's Germany are direct descendants of century's old entities, conserved more or less whole (Bavaria, Hamburg) or expanded (Hesse, Saxony) or restored (Schleswig-Holstein). Other Länder originate in the fusion of ancient entities (Baden-Württemberg, Mecklenburg-Western Pomerania), and others still derive from the division of the ancient Prussian territory in more defined regions, motivated by historical, geographical and economic reasons.

This structure is based on an interweaving of historical, geographic, and economic factors, while not emphasizing one over the other. It allows for the transfer to the individual federal entities, the ethical-political aspects of the idea of citizenship, as belonging to a larger civil community. Precisely because of this, such a structure does not damage, and in fact reinforces the identity of the German nation as a whole. Its continuity is required by the German Governments as a precondition for a future European Union. It is also and particularly in Germany that the idea of a regional and national double identity and a double political participation has made headway. Will the progress of a European union make a triple identity possible?

# 9

## Italy

Two conceptions of territory compared

There are many historical similarities between Germany and Italy.

Italy also belonged to the heart of the medieval empire, enjoyed a precocious developments of its cities, and therefore paid the price of political annihilation. Italy was also overrun by expanding nation-states on the Western side of the continent, and its territories became an arena for games of balance of power. Italy was also a theater for the expansion of the Napoleonic armies, which created ephemeral unifications, and new orders. In 1815, the re-establishment of pre-Revolutionary conditions brought simpli-fication and incorporation of new territories: great states like the Republic of Venice and the Republic of Genoa were not reconstituted. Italy of 1815 consisted of territories of very different capacities and institutional forms.

Since the propagation of the ideas of the French revolution, the dilemma of types of unification and national borders was felt strongly in Italy. In Italy, top-down unification also prevailed over unification from the bottom-up. It happened through expansion and incorporation around an antecedent state: Piedmont, or the Kingdom of Sardinia. The historical and geographical location of this state was as peripheral as that of Prussia, which had originated the German Empire.

Italian unification took about as long as German unification. Italy was also intertwined with the European powers: the war of 1866 between Prussia and Austria allowed Italy to annex Veneto; the war between Prussia and France created an auspicious occasion for taking Rome. Italy inherited multi-ethnic conflicts, particularly in territories with a majority, or a presence, of Germans, Slovenians, and Croats, annexed in 1919. Italy also suffered a burning defeat in World War II, losing ethnically Italian areas such as Pola, Fiume, and Zara.

Unlike Germany, though, the Italian union of 1861 did not keep the antecedent states. On the contrary, Italy was constituted through progressive annexation of various states, and territories of the Kingdom of Sardinia, which, in many respects, continued to exist in the new state. Austria gave Lombardy to the Kingdom of Sardinia through an international treaty. Emilia, Tuscany, Umbria, the Marches, and the *Mezzogiorno* ratified the annexation with plebiscites of unconditional union: the survival of laws or particular institutions was neither guaranteed, nor taken into consideration. Along with the judicial system, the Piedmontese, centralized model of administration—directly modeled on the Napoleonic model—was extended to Lombardy and the other states. The first-level territorial units became the provinces, administered by governors nominated by the king. They would later be called Prefects, French-style. In 1860 and 1861, Luigi Carlo Farini, Marco Minghetti, and Gustavo Ponza di San Martino debated territorial reform for the new state. They underlined the need to introduce a larger, autonomous unit: the region. Regions were to have a double aim: to retain the particularities of the Lombard, Tuscan, and Emilian states, and to assist in the integration of the Kingdom of Naples—so different in history and organization. But the reform collapsed. By 1865, a process of complete homogenization of the state's organization was concluded.

The issue of the territorial model of the Italian state became topical again in 1945. This was partly triggered by the recognition that the state's ethnic lay-out was far from simple.

Italy's ethnic structure conforms to the polarized model which characterizes France and Spain. In Italy, many ethnic minorities (but not all) are located near borders. In the Western area, on France's border, Occitanean and Franco-Provençal dialects are spoken: not just in the Val d'Aosta, but in many valleys of Piedmont. The borders between Switzerland and Austria are characterized by a compact area of Germans in the *Alto Adige/Südtirol* and by many areas—dispersed in various regions—with archaic German dialects, traces of medieval migrations. The area of Slovenian language, on the other hand, extends on the west of the border into the provinces of Udine, Gorizia and Trieste. It is in the areas adjacent to Austria and Slovenia that Friulano and Ladino Dolomite are spoken, considered by linguists to be two autonomous Neolatin languages, or variations on a single language.

At the end of the World War II, the possibility for ethnic tension was increased by the fact that the fascist regime had engaged in a politics of forced normalization, repressing minority languages. In different ways and with different intensities, secessionist proposals emerged in Valle D'Aosta, Alto Adige, and in the border area with Slovenia. France and Yugoslavia had won the war. Austria, on the other hand, remembered the iniquities of the borders of 1919.

Immediately after the war, Italy guaranteed not only the integrity of part of its Alpine borders, but also the defusing of potential ethnic conflicts by the creation of autonomous regions, with a vast number of jurisdictions. In 1947, Trentino-Alto Adige was instituted; in 1948, Valle D'Aosta; in 1963 Friuli-Venezia Giulia. In 1972, Trentino-Alto Adige was divided into the autonomous provinces of Trento and Bolzano. To the same period, immediately after the war, we date the regional autonomy of Sicily (1946) and Sardinia (1948), recognizing very particular historical identities (which for Sardinia is also an ethno-linguistic identity).

Italy's regional reform dates to 1970, with the creation of the assemblies and governments of 15 other regions (with "ordinary statute"). After nearly twenty years, the decentralization of Italy continues. It is considered a means by which to confront the present political, economic, and planning crises. Many look with interest towards the German Federalist constitution. In 1993, the bicameral commission for institutional reform approved a project which reverses the meaning of article 117 of the present constitution: instead of defining the jurisdictions of the regions and deferring the rest to the state, the procedure starts by defining the jurisdictions of the state and deferring everything else to the regions.

The problem is that this regionalist reform is fought against by those who, apparently because of the same need to help local communities, propose the elimination of the present order, and the creation of new identities defined as "macro-regions," which would divide the Italian state into three great geographic strata: a Northern, Central, and Southern macro-region.

There is only one point of agreement between the two plans. That is the conservation of the six autonomous entities (considering Bolzano and Trento separately). The six entities, nevertheless, cover only 24.7% of the area and 15.5% of the population. For the rest, which involves 226,790 Km$^2$ and 47,959,433 inhabitants, the opinions couldn't differ more. To divide Italy into fifteen parts or into three parts requires quite different logics.

Let us compare the two alternative territorial arrangements. For the sake of simplicity we have assumed that the borders of the macro-regions are the same as today's regional borders. The North would include Piedmont, Liguria, Lombardy, Veneto, Emilia-Romagna; the Center Tuscany, Umbria, the Marches, Lazio; the South, Campania, Molise, Puglia, Basilicata, Calabria. We have considered only one case controversial, that of Abruzzo. Historical reasons would place it in the South (it was traditionally a part of the Kingdom of Naples), present-day economic reasons (the Rome-Pescara axis) would place it in the Center. We have therefore presented two different "macro-regional" arrangements: in hypothesis A, Abruzzo is included with the Center; in B, with the South.

| Italy with 21 Regions | Area (Km²) | Population (1991) |
|---|---|---|
| Sicily | 25,707 | 4,966,386 |
| Piedmont | 25,339 | 4,302,565 |
| Sardinia | 24,090 | 1,648,248 |
| Lombardy | 23,859 | 8,856,074 |
| Tuscany | 22,992 | 3,529,946 |
| Emilia-Romagna | 22,125 | 3,909,512 |
| Puglia | 19,357 | 4,031,885 |
| Veneto | 18,365 | 4,380,797 |
| Lazio | 17,227 | 5,140,371 |
| Calabria | 15,080 | 2,070,203 |
| Campania | 13,595 | 5,630,280 |
| Abruzzo | 10,794 | 1,249,054 |
| Basilicata | 9,992 | 610,528 |
| The Marches | 9,693 | 1,429,205 |
| Umbria | 8,456 | 811,831 |
| Friuli-Venezia-Giulia | 7,844 | 1,197,666 |
| Bolzano | 7,400 | 440,508 |
| Trento | 6,207 | 449,852 |
| Liguria | 5,418 | 1,676,282 |
| Molise | 4,438 | 330,900 |
| Valle D'Aosta | 3,264 | 115,938 |
| Total | 301,302 | 56,778,031 |

If we use the present German arrangement as a comparison, the two Italian arrangements (regions or macro-regions) are seen to be at opposite sides of the coin.

The plan with 21 regions is more decentralized than the German plan. The largest region (Sicily) comprises of 8.5% of the national territory, and the sum of the two largest regions (Sicily and Piedmont) comprises 16.9%; the most highly populated region

(Lombardy) comprises of 15.6% of the entire population, while the sum of the two most highly populated regions (Lombardy and Campania) makes up 25.5%.

The data for the macro regional plan are very different. The North in any case both the largest and the most densely populated region) on its own makes up 31.6% of the area and 40.7% of the population. The sum of the two largest regions climbs to 54.5% (North and Center, hypothesis A) or 55.9% (North and South, hypothesis B). The sum of the two most highly populated regions (North and South, in any case) climbs to 63.1% (hypothesis A) or 65.3% (hypothesis B).

*Macro-regions*

| | Hypothesis A | | Hypothesis B | |
|---|---|---|---|---|
| | *Area* | *Population* | *Area* | *Population* |
| North | 95,166 | 23,125,230 | 95,166 | 23,125,230 |
| Center | 69,162 | 12,160,407 | 58,368 | 10,911,353 |
| South | 62,462 | 12,673,796 | 73,256 | 13,922,850 |
| Sicily | 25,707 | 4,966,386 | 25,707 | 4,966,386 |
| Sardinia | 24,,090 | 1,648,248 | 24,090 | 1,648,248 |
| Friuli-V. G. | 7,844 | 1,197,666 | 7,844 | 1,197,666 |
| Bolzano | 7,400 | 440,508 | 7,400 | 440,508 |
| Trento | 6,207 | 449,852 | 6,207 | 449,852 |
| Valle D'Aosta | 3,264 | 115,938 | 6,207 | 449,852 |
| *Total* | 301,302 | 56,778,031 | 301,302 | 56,778,031 |

Always following the parameters of the German plan, we shall see that *all three* macro-regions can be compared in terms of size only to the largest Land, Bavaria: in hypothesis A, in fact, all three macro-regions exceed the area percentage of Bavaria in the overall area of the German Federal Republic. And, as for population, all three macro-regions can be compared only to the most highly populated Land, Rheinland-Northern Westfalia: in both hypotheses, North and South exceed the relative percentage.

Compared to the criteria used by the German plan, therefore, the three Italian macro-regions would appear very large and populous.

This impression is confirmed if we examine the administrative units of the other Western European states, also engaged, albeit with different objectives, in a regional reform of their territory. In Spain, the three largest autonomous communities are, in effect, comparable in area to the three Italian macro-regions: Castille-León (94.222 Km$^2$), Andalusia (87.598 Km$^2$), Castille-La Mancha (76.491 Km$^2$). But Spain is considerably larger than Italy, and the effect on the overall territory is therefore much smaller: 18.6% for Castille-León, 35.9% for Castille-León + Andalusia (figures which compare well to the German arrangement). As far as population is concerned, in any case, the orders of relative magnitude are similar: 17.9% for the most highly populated region, Andalusia (which only has 6,859,958 inhabitants); 33.4% for Andalusia and Catalonia.

The relative area of the French regions, on the other hand, is generally smaller than both the German Länder and the Spanish autonomous communities. The largest region (Midi-Pyrénées, 45.348 Km$^2$), takes up 8.3% of the overall French territory; the two largest regions (Midi-Pyrénées + Rhone-Alps), 16.4%. The most highly populated region (Paris, Ile-de-France) numbers 10,660,554 inhabitants, 18.8% of the total: added to the second most populated region, we get 28.3%. For population and territory, the figures for France, are closer to today's Italy.

Let us review the relevant figures for the two alternative orderings of Italy (Italy 1: regions; Italy 2: macro-regions—if necessary with figures added for hypotheses A and B) comparing them to France, Spain, and Germany.

| | Italy 1 | France | Spain | Germany | Italy 2 |
|---|---|---|---|---|---|
| Number of units | 21 | 22 | 17 | 16 | 9 |
| Average area (Km$^2$) per unit | 14,348 | 24,726 | 29762 | 22303 | 33478 |
| Average population per unit | 2,703,716 | 2,573,386 | 2,260,334 | 4,964,577 | 6,308,670 |
| Area relative to the largest unit | 8.5 | 8.3 | 18.6 | 19.8 | 31.6 |
| Area relative to the *two* largest units | 16.9 | 16.4 | 35.9 | 33 | 54.5/55.9 |
| Area relative to the *three* largest units | 24.9 | 24 | 51.1 | 43.1 | 75.3 |
| Population compared to the most highly populated unit | 15.6 | 18.8 | 17.9 | 21.8 | 40.7 |
| Population compared to the *two* most highly populated units | 25.5 | 28.3 | 33.4 | 36.1 | 63.1/65.3 |
| Population compared to the *three* most highly populated units | 34.6 | 35.8 | 46 | 48.4 | 84.5 |

Germany, France, and Spain have enacted their reforms over different periods of time, in different situations, and with different objectives. They have given the new units vastly different jurisdictions and degrees of freedom of action, which at times vary even within the same system. On one point, nevertheless, they seem to converge. Their units are multiple, balanced, and never exceed relatively small thresholds of population and territory. All in all, they represent a decentralization of decision-making. Comparing these experiments, one could see emerging a real Europe of regions, in which the subsidiarity principle included in the Maastricht treaty brings citizens closer to centers of power, making them participants in a civic culture of communities which are sufficiently agile and flexible.

The present-day Italian regions fit into such a scheme. Perhaps it will be useful to incorporate some of the smaller regions, perhaps the birth of some new local identities.

On the other hand, the Italy of macro-regions does not fit into this scheme.

The Italy of macro-regions seems to outline a project of centering and secondary centralization, through the hypothetical inclusion of a large part of a large and populous national territory into three large and populous units. Let us remember that the 23 million inhabitants of the republic of the North would place her, alone, in seventh place among the most populated European countries, behind Germany, France, Great Britain, Ukraine, Poland, and Spain, and in front of Rumania and the Netherlands. (Of course, this does not include Italy or the Euro-Asiatic countries of Russia and Asia.) Right behind her would be the two republics of the Center and the South. In both the hypotheses we have presented, the Center and the South would have a population larger than Hungary, Yugoslavia (Serbia + Montenegro), the Czech Republic, Byelorussia, Greece, Belgium, Portugal, and Sweden.... The internal structure of the macro-regional Italy would startlingly resemble Germany in 1871 or 1918, with a slightly more restricted Prussia, a slightly broader Bavaria, and the inclusion of some central states....

In any case, the regions would be the primary victims of a macro-regional Italy. Two possible scenarios present themselves. According to the first scenario, the present regions (the 15 "ordinarie") would be reduced to second level administrative units. Above them would be a state apparatus and moreover a macro-regional apparatus. We can believe that the federal reform could slim down the first apparatus in favor of the second, but this would always increase bureaucracy and the clash of competencies. In a second scenario, the present regions would be remodeled in favor of, possibly, smaller and more manageable second-level units. In that case, the structure would be very reminiscent not only of Prussian centralism, but also of some socialist countries....

The fundamental point, nevertheless, is this: neither the ethnic nor the historical roots of the Italian nation in any way justify a separation into three enormous units, in the north, middle, and south of the peninsula. On the contrary, the nation's multiplicity and plurality of roots seem better served precisely by today's arrangement.

It is interesting to note that, linguistically, while the Neolatin languages of France and Spain have, in fact, created linguistic polarizations between North and South (French/Occitanian) and North-East and South-West (Catalan/Castillian), most Italian dialects have continued—since the High Middle Ages—to be part of a single language, from which only Sardinian, Friulian, and Dolomite Ladino have become distinguished.

Linguists have identified phonetic and morphological borders between the various types of Italian dialects: these borders basically divide into three groups: the dialects of the North, the Tuscan dialects, and those dialects which extend over the rest of Italy and a good part of the South. But starting with this basic picture, soon a communicative circle emerged, in which from the dialects emerged a national language made up of many different dialects, and in turn the national language has "retro-acted" on the dialects, transforming them. The principal source of the Italian literary language has been the Tuscan dialects. But, since its origins, it has been open to other influences, coming above all from the Po Valley: the humanist Bembo could say that "the language of Dante often sounds more like Lombard than Tuscan." And since its origins the literary language forged in Tuscany exercised a decisive influence not only on written norms, but also on the languages spoken in Venice and Rome. On the other hand, the dialects of Sicily and southern Calabria are not at all of a southern type, but rather of a northern one, because they derive from migrations which transformed the region's population after the Byzantine and Arab ages.

The variety of Italian dialects is not the result of separation, but of reciprocal circulation and communication. As a consequence, the development of an Italian national culture has followed a multiplicity of itineraries, not just vertically, but also horizontally and transversally.

Historically, only Southern Italy has been characterized for many centuries by a single, largely uninterrupted political unity, even if in a territory with difficult internal communication.

The center was pulverized in the Middle Ages, and then progressively remodeled by the two attractor poles of Florence and Rome, which in the modern age have practically divided amongst themselves the entire territory.

As for the North—the unit that presents itself largest and most compact in the project of the macro-regions—it is precisely the Italian area that has been most diversified politically over the centuries. In the first centuries after 1000, Northern Italy followed the other regions of the empire and was territorially pulverized. It then assembled itself around many centers (Milan, Genoa, Turin, Parma, Modena, Venezia...) which never exercised supremacy over each other.

Other historical aspects are worth noting. In the first place, the borders of what we call the Italian regional states are always changing, and this has created many areas where one can find numerous different local identities superimposed. Lombardy, for example, has followed the destiny of Milan to a great extent, but was unified completely only in the few years of Napoleonic dominion and after Italy was united. Distinct from those of central Lombardy are the travails of Northern Lombardy (Lomellina) which has often followed the fate of Piedmont; or Eastern Lombardy (Bergamo, Brescia), which has followed the fate of Venice; or Mantova, which for centuries has maintained an autonomous identity.... Secondly, a part of the political communities of the North have also been ex-centric, they have, in other words, brought together for centuries, territories and cultures located even outside the geographic and national limits of Italy. We think of Piedmont (integrated for centuries by the Savoy dynasty in a state astride the Alps, between French and Italian cultures), of the association of Genoa with Corsica, to the Venetian Republic's horizons in Istria, Dalmatia, Greece and the Aegean, to the profound integration of Trieste and Trento in the affairs of the Germanic world, and the Danubian world....

The regions respect this complexity better than the macro-regions. The regions bring to light the many relations Italy has with many areas of Europe better than the macro-regions: with the Neo-latin world, the Germanic world, the Slavic world, even the world of the Balkans. Circulation and communication against separation; the image of a polycentric web against the hierarchization around three centers; continuity with respect to historical identity against a simplification and rewriting of history, which, in the end, assumes as its only criterion the presumption of economic development. In Italy's present institutional crisis, there are at stake not insignificant differences in values, and contrasting appeals to the imagination.

# 10

## From the Baltic to the Black Sea

### Competing ethnicities

In 1815, the central band of Europe was marked by the political pulverization of the two great German and Italian ethnicities. The Eastern band of Europe was in the exact opposite position: a few, immense state powers governed many ethnicities. There were certainly many communities which in some way or other were able to avoid direct government by these state entities. The Congress of Vienna had made Krakow a free city, stuck between Austria, Russia, and Prussia, the final residue of a once splendid Poland, annihilated by the partitions of the previous century. In the southwestern Balkans, in some mountains and some valleys of Montenegro, life was more or less independent of the circumstances of the Ottoman Empire. Farther north, certain principalities (Serbia, Wallachia, Moldavia) enjoyed a certain degree of autonomy from the sovereign in Constantinople. But it is doubtful that these entities could be considered states, subject to international law. In any event, Krakow was annexed by Austria in 1846.

The three great multi-national empires (the Austrian, Ottoman, and Russian) and eastern Prussia divided the entire scene among themselves. In the three multi-national empires, the dominant political ethnicities— German, Russian, and Turkish—were not the absolute majority. Unlike what was happening in central western Europe, the three empires had no national majority, but only minorities involved in a game of domination and emancipation.

Most of the minority ethnic groups had a strong feeling of national identity, which could be traced to political entities which had flourished in the Middle Ages, or in the first centuries of the Modern Age. For the Poles and Lithuanians, the memory of a common state created with the Union of Lublin in 1569 was still vivid. The Czechs founded their sense of identity upon the Kingdom of Bohemia which, while subject to the Germans, experienced centuries continuity under the Holy Roman Empire. Even more ancient were the memories of Hungarians, Serbs, Croats and Montenegrins. The memories of Orthodox Ukrainians had their roots in the great state of Kiev, which had its apogee in the XIth century. The name Bulgaria could be traced back as far as 681, when the new people, a mixture of Slavs, Turks, and Thracians, became independent of Byzantium for the first time.

Other ethnicities (Estonians, Slovakians, Byelorussians, Ruthenians, Slovenians) had not enjoyed such extensive political successes, and had been part of states or multi-national empires. The formation of their national consciousness was marked by the important role of a written language based on oral traditions and local dialects.

Even if often tied to a common struggle for emancipation from multi-national empires, misunderstandings and incomprehension between the two types of ethnicities were frequent. Basing themselves on history, many ethnicities claimed "natural" rights to the possession of this or that territory, rights which were in turn not recognized by bordering ethnicities. When the Hungarians obtained the right to self-government within the Habsburg Empire, they distinguished themselves in their attempt to assimilate the ethnicities they incorporated.

In 1815, only a few of the various ethnicities in east-central Europe were divided into areas with a compact population, so that they could stoke the fires and be a point of reference for this or that national movement. In most cases, the ethno-linguistic borders were broken up, and interrupted by many linguistic islands and by cities and regions populated by many ethnicities. Only a few ethnicities were almost completely contained in a small territory. Other ethnicities, being the majority in a particular territory, had been pushed by historical events into other regions, where they were minorities.

Both Prussia and Austrian were crossed by the border between German and Slav Europe: in the preceding centuries, Germans had settled to the East (on Baltic coast), and Slavs had remained in the West (in Bohemia, by the Oder). The push of the *Drang nach Osten* had spread German colonies throughout east central Europe, settling in territories with Slav majorities (or Magyar, Baltic, or Romanian). On the other hand, the ethnic borders between the Slavs themselves were even less clear, because often, in the absence of precise written norms, many transitional, un-individualized dialects were spoken. Even in the first half of this century, in the eastern territories of Poland, there lived a mixture of Poles, Byelorussians, Ukrainians, and Rutens (Catholic Ukrainians), to which belonged also Silesian farmers known as *tutajszy* (in Polish: "those who are from here") because they answered the census's question about the language they spoke by saying "the local dialect." In this century, heated linguistic and political debates have developed around the question of whether the Macedonian of the Skopje area, which originated in transitional dialects between Serb and Bulgarian, should be brought together with Serb or Bulgarian.

Eastern central Europe was also the land of Diaspora: gypsies; Jews persecuted in the West (the Yiddish-speaking Ashkenazi Jews had left Germany looking for refuge in the East, after the pogroms which followed the Black Plague in 1348; the Spanish-speaking Sephardic Jews had settled in the Balkans, after 1492); colonizers (Germans in the Baltic countries, Turks in the Balkans, Circassians in Moldavia, Russians in Ukraine); merchants (since antiquity, Greeks populated the ports of all the coasts of the Black Sea, followed in many places by Armenians around the time of the Ottoman Empire). In the eighteenth century, other Diaspora of farmers were added, looking for new lands to escape the misery of an over-populated central Europe. Catherine of Russia, German by birth, had called many German colonizers along the banks of the Volga, in Ukraine, in the Caucasus, to modernize agriculture, to farm virgin territories, to re-populate lands which had recently been torn from the Turks. The Habsburg Emperors Charles VI and Marie Theresa had behaved in a similar manner. In order to cultivate and preside over the thin strip of land conquered in the Balkans, at the expense of the retreating Ottoman Empire, they had called in Croatia, Slavonia, Backa, and Banat, peoples of all nationalities of the Habsburgian dominion, and even Serbs who sought better conditions than those under the Ottomans. Many of these Serbs settled close to the coasts of Dalmatia, in Western Croatia, in the region that to this day is known as *Krajina* (border).

After 1815, the legacy of the French Revolution changed the scenario of the Balkans profoundly. The élites of the Christian peoples began to look to Paris with interest, seeing there a place where a nation-state and a national citizenship had been forged. They thought the time had come to profit from the weakness of the Ottoman Empire to allow the situation to evolve in a manner consonant with their aspirations. But the successes of the French Revolution had been the outpouring of a process that had started centuries earlier; the monarchy had made a profound effort to transform a purely territorial state, made up of heterogeneous regions and different habits, into a nation-state, sharing a common administration, culture, language, and social imaginary. In the Balkans, on the contrary, the expansion of the Ottomans had created a clear discontinuity with the preceding centuries and now the reaction of the nations promised to create an equally clear discontinuity.

To defend their rights, and in order to legitimate their aspirations, the national élites of the Christian ethnic groups of the Balkans (Serbs, Bulgarians, Rumanians, Greeks) engaged in a task of reconstructing and revivifying the memories and traditions of the pre-Ottoman past, of which they proclaimed themselves the heirs. The Serbs' memory went back to the Kingdom of Stefan Dusan, which, with Skopje as the capital, extended from the Adriatic to the Aegean seas. Twice, in the Middle Ages, the Bulgarians had created a great empire, on territories harshly contested with the empire of Constantinople. The Neo-Latin language allowed Romanians to go back to the colonization of Dacia by the Romans. As for the Greeks, memory called them to the same empire of Constantinople, to the oriental empire which from 395 to 1453 had been a constant presence in the region. In this genealogical research, the Greeks were the most fortunate. Alongside the medieval identity, another more ancient and more illustrious heritage was rediscovered and brought to the fore: Classical Greece. In reality, its memory was all but gone from the Hellenic peninsula and the Aegean islands. But it remained, indelible, in the whole of European culture, and above all in the learned circles of the Western countries. The richness of the Greek people's roots aided the satisfaction of her national aspirations. France and England were particularly sensitive to her remote past. The Russian Empire, on the other hand, assisted her largely because she belonged to the community of Orthodox religions.

In this search for genealogies, religion always played an important part. Greeks, Serbs, Montenegrins, Bulgarians, Romanians, were and are, almost completely, of the Orthodox faith. In the centuries of Ottoman occupation, the Eastern Greek Church extended its civil and spiritual jurisdiction over all these peoples, in the context of the *millet* system, and became the decisive factor for the transmission and conservation of their identity. Moreover, although the patriarch of Constantinople was the authority recognized by the Ottomans as the head of the Orthodox nation, since the Middle Ages Serbs and Bulgarians had had national Churches *autocephalous* each with its own patriarch, and not subordinated in matters of religion to the patriarch of Constantinople (who was more like a *primus inter pares*). In the Balkans, in the last century (and even in this century), religious persuasion was superimposed on and intertwined with ethnic identity in an inextricable knot.

The fact that Greek and Serb meant Orthodox, was considered necessary and inevitable.

In Serbia, the importance of religious identity had slowed the development of a national language. The liturgical language, ancient ecclesiastical Slav, kept a great deal of literary prestige. The dialects of daily life were strictly oral. In the realm of linguistics, the initiative fell above all to the Croats. They were the most inclined toward a fusion of Southern Slav peoples and promoted a literary language half-way between Zagreb and Belgrade, half-way between the Slavs of the Habsburg Empire and the Slavs of the Ottoman Empire. Voluntarily forfeiting particularities, some Croat writers renounced their native language, from the region of Zagreb, to adopt the dialect of Herzegovina, the most suitable for the linguistic unification of the largest possible area. Serbo-Croat was born, a common language which nevertheless continued to be written in two different alphabets: the Latin alphabet in Croatia, the Cyrillic in Serbia and Montenegro. But linguistic unification did not produce the ethnic unification of Orthodox Serbs and Catholic Croats. On the contrary, Serbs and Croats remained tenaciously attached to their quite divergent stories and memories, often to the point of conflict.

After 1815, one of the first crises for the new Europe was generated by the question of Greek independence. All Europe mobilized to uphold Greek rights and obtain a nation-state. In 1830, the Ottomans recognized the new state, which included the Peloponnesus, the region of Athens, Boetia, Etolia, Eubea, the Cyclads, and other islands of the western Aegean. Despite this, Greek aspirations were not completely satisfied. Beyond the borders of the new state, much more restricted than today's, there remained ample clusters of Hellenic population. The new direction in Greek politics became the *Megáli Idéa*: to reunite in the motherland all these areas, and perhaps other areas which had belonged to the Byzantine domains. Istanbul itself became the ultimate goal of the *Megáli Idéa*.

The Greeks became an example in the area. Serbs, Rumanians, and Bulgarians began to conceive of great projects of territorial expansion. Nevertheless, the European powers continued for decades in a complicated game, which involved fueling, controlling, and, at the same time, breaking the nationalist aspirations of the Balkan people. Serbia, Montenegro, and Rumania obtained the rights to degrees of ever greater self-government, but in relatively small territories. In any case, their formula for association with the Ottoman authorities was not always clear and not always respected.

# 11

## Macedonia

### The balkanization of the Balkans

Eighteen seventy-seven was a watershed year. Russia saw that the time was right to profit from the crumbling Ottoman Empire, to take an active part in the Balkans, to try to control passage through the Bosphorus and perhaps to go beyond it, into the Mediterranean. The national aspirations of the Bulgarians allowed it to intervene as an intermediary. After a victorious war, the Russians imposed the Peace of St. Stephen on the Ottomans. The conditions were extremely heavy. They were not only forced to recognize the independence of Bulgaria, but had to give her a large part of their European territories. The Bulgaria of St. Stephen was much larger than today's Bulgaria: it had an outlet on the Mediterranean, and, above all, it possessed almost the entire region that to this day is known as Macedonia: it reached all the way to Skopje, in the valley of the Vardar, and reached lands populated by Greeks and Albanians. Bulgaria essentially captured a large part of today's independent Macedonia, and Greek Macedonia. The double connection that tied the Bulgarians to the Czar's empire worried the other powers. These powers pressured Russia for a new compromise at the Congress of Berlin. The collective decisions would have guaranteed a more balanced order, with respect to both the sphere of influence of the great powers and the relationship between the new nation-states and the ancient Ottoman Empire. Bulgaria was demoted to the rank of autonomous principality, in a much more restricted territory (smaller than today's) and still within the domain of the Ottoman Empire. As compensation, territorial advantages and promotions in status were recognized to other ethnicities and states: Serbia, Montenegro, and Greece. Vast regions were returned to the Ottoman Empire. It remained an important presence on European soil: it possessed Thrace, the whole of Macedonia, Kosovo, today's Albania, and today's southern Bulgaria (which, already in 1885, had largely been taken back by the Bulgarians). To counterbalance the Russian influence, furthermore, Austria-Hungary occupied the eastern-most territory of the ancient Ottoman domains: Bosnia-Herzegovina. It was a fatal error.

The centers in which new Balkan states were born and developed (the nuclei of Greece, Serbia, Montenegro, and Bulgaria) were ethnically relatively homogeneous. In part, their new acquisitions were also homogeneous in 1878.

The same cannot be said for the part the Ottomans continued to control. An inextricable ethnic mix had been generated over the centuries by the most disparate events: the colonization of the Ottoman victors, the flight of the losers, migration of the farmers, fear of epidemics.

The term Macedonia became proverbial at that point in the whole of Europe, and came into the western languages to mean a mixed-fruit salad. In this area the Muslim element was also very strong. There were in fact many Turkish colonies, which had settled centuries earlier; many territories populated by Albanians, who had largely converted to Islam; many Slav centers, which had also been conquered by the imperial religion (like the Pomars, Bulgarian-speaking but of Muslim faith). This area was host to vast communities of Sephardic Jews, who in the city of Salonika represented a relative majority. In many mountain regions, the Wallachian farmers were numerous, speaking a language close to Romanian, which the distance from their nation-state was forcing into a steady decline.

But, above all, the area was populated by individual collectivities of ethnicities identical or related to the three bordering nations: Serbia, Greece, Bulgaria. For different reasons, all three aspired to possess the greater part of the European territory that was still in the hands of the Ottoman Empire. All three were furiously developing reasons and arguments to claim their rights. But if these reasons seemed good, they weren't strong enough. In any case, the reasons of one nation inevitably came into conflict with the reasons of another. An illuminating and curious testament to this conflict are the statistics which at the end of the last century were kept by Greeks, Serbs, and Bulgarians, all with the intention of showing that rights to the whole of Macedonia belonged only to them. Rather than revealing intentional fraud, these statistics show how unilateral and tendentious the approach to ethnic and national questions sometimes is.

| Ethnicities | Bulgarian Statistics (1900) | Greek Statistics (1904, not including Kosovo) | Serb Statistics (1889) |
|---|---|---|---|
| Turks | 499,200 | 634,000 | 231,000 |
| Albanians | 128,700 | — | 165,000 |
| Bulgarians | 1,181,000 | 332,000 | 57,600 |
| Serbs | 700 | — | 2,048,000 |
| Greeks | 228,7000 | 652,700 | 201,100 |
| Wallachians | 80,700 | 25,100 | 69,000 |
| Jews | 67,800 | 53,100 | 64,600 |
| Gypsies | 54,500 | 8,900 | 28,700 |
| Other | 16,500 | 18,600 | 3,500 |
| Total | 2,258,000 | 1,724,000 | 2,870,000 |

The statistics of Greeks, Bulgarians, and Serbs had only one thing in common. Every time, the nation proposing the statistics claimed to be in the majority in the territory being claimed: only a relative majority for the Greeks (37.9%), absolute for the Bulgarians (52.3%) and for the Serbs (71.4%). At the same time, the competing ethnicities vanished (the Serbs were insignificant for the Bulgarians, and did not even exist for the Greeks!) or were considerably reduced.

But two deep and not at all contingent reasons explain what might at first appear to be a game of prestige.

The first reason is as follows: the idea of nationality had not yet become autonomous from religious criteria, which we saw being the only pertinent factor for the Ottoman Empire. Indeed, for the Ottomans, in Macedonia there were essentially only three groups, defined on the basis of faith: Muslims (1,145,000), Orthodox Greeks subject to the patriarchate of Constantinople (623,000), and Orthodox Bulgarians (626,000), subject to their autonomous exarchate which had been restored in 1870. Among the Muslims, for instance, there were not only Turks, but Albanians, Circassians, Gypsies, and a number of Greeks, Bulgarians, Slavs, Persians, and converted Jews (Donmë). The Greek statistics were largely built around a similar scheme.

Then there was a second problem: the introduction of a certain kind of linguistic criterion facilitated the individuation of non-Slavic ethnicities (Albanians, Greeks, Turks) and the separation of Slavic from non-Slavic ethnicities (Bulgarians from Greeks, for example), but did not resolve problems of individuation and distinction in the population of Slavic language and culture.

Earlier, there had been no rigid boundaries between Slovenian and Bulgarian languages, only a series of dialects connected and separated by concords and discords. In the western area of the Balkans, the emergence of a precise Croat norm (and therefore Serb-Croatian) had progressively distanced the Slovenian languages from the alpine regions, which in turn became the nucleus of a new autonomous language. More to the south, on the other hand, in the nineteenth century the situation was still fluid. Two clearly distinct languages, the Serbian language (Serbo-Croatian) and the Bulgarian language were already formed. But in the vast intermediate area, many dialects presented characteristics which might indicate to which of the two they would belong, not merely on purely linguistic criteria, but also for more general ends conceived as they went along. This allowed the Serbs to try to annex to their language all the transitional Macedonian dialects, which were no doubt considered Bulgarian by eastern competitors. More detached linguists proposed a third possibility: the transitional dialects presented autonomous characteristics, which could have become the nucleus for a new literary language. For the German geographer Oestreich, in 1905, Macedonia was populated not by Serbs or by Bulgarians, but by Slavo-Macedonians, numbering around 2 million.

In the last decades of the nineteenth century and the first decade of the twentieth, Serbs, Bulgarians, Greeks and even Rumanians fought over influence in Macedonia with national churches, schools, cultural societies, railways, and history lessons. At times they used more drastic methods, and resorted to physical elimination. Others dissociated themselves from the interested voices of their neighbors. They felt themselves to be an autonomous nationality, and coined the slogan "Macedonia for Macedonians." In 1903, the separatists defended for forty days an embryonic republic.

In the first years of the century, the attacks of terrorism in the name of independence and the Ottoman repressions increased. The situation was on the verge of becoming explosive, because at that point two conflicts were irreconcilably intertwined: that of the Christian nations against the Ottoman Empire, and of the Christian nations against each other. And two conflicts did take place, when, in 1912, the crises feared by many broke out. All together, the Balkan states succeeded in fighting the Turks back to the gates of Istanbul, tearing all the European lands away from them. But the

Macedonian question immediately raised the fiercest discord in their camp. With the strength of weapons, the Bulgarians had built for themselves a space that was similar to the Peace of St. Stephen: in particular, they held a vast stretch of the Mediterranean coast. For the Greeks and Serbs, the situation seemed intolerable. They allied with Turks and Romanians to change the balance once again. The new coalition prevailed, and the allies managed to contain Bulgarian expansion. The Turks returned partly to European soil, retaking possession of eastern Thrace, which they hold to this day. Today we are discovering the relevance of the stories told of these wars by many western observers: they spoke of atrocities and ethnic massacres, by all involved, almost identical to those being committed in the same area seventy years later.

The intervention of the great powers brought peace, but only made the situation more intricate. On the coast of the Adriatic, on the western part of the old Ottoman dominion, a new people obtained independence: the Albanians. But the state was much smaller than the area in which Albanians were the majority. Between the original Albanian proposal, which aspired to territories that were not ethnically Albanian, and the Serbo-Greco-Montenegrin proposal, which wanted a tiny state so that they could divide up the rest, a compromise border was chosen, very similar to today's. A good part of ethnic Albanian territory, a large part of Kosovo and western Macedonia, went to Serbia.

The situation was already explosive when a new crisis exploded in another region with an inextricable ethnic mixture: Bosnia-Herzegovina.

# 12

## Yugoslavia

### A microcosm of the century

Among the many ethnic problems inherited by the partition of the Ottoman possessions, the Albanian question was by no means insignificant. Twice, in 1878 and 1913, Serbia became larger, annexing territories inhabited by Muslim populations: Albanians, Turks, and Islamic Slavs (who spoke Serbian or Macedonian dialects). In 1878, the annexed territory was populated by a Serb majority. Not so during the war maneuvers of 1912 and the complicated arrangement of 1913: in Kosovo, Albanians were clearly in the majority.

Relations between Serbians and Albanians became very tense. Albanians had obtained their nation-state. But it was a poor state, small, and above all frustrated, because aspirations of uniting the entire Albanian nation under one flag had only partially been satisfied. It was inevitable that many Albanians of Kosovo should aspire to being included, sooner or later, within the borders of their motherland.

The fact that, at that moment, Albanians were a distinct majority in Kosovo did not make Serbians' feelings about that newly annexed region less strong. Kosovo had been one of the fundamental centers of the kingdom of Stefan Dusan, the source of legitimacy for the new state. It had also been the theater of an epic battle, in 1389, from which the Serbs, although defeated, continued to derive sustenance for their newly won identity. In the partition of 1913, furthermore, Montenegro received an adjacent area, also populated largely by Albanians, which was perhaps more important for the identity of Serbs. Saint Sava, founder of the Serbian National church had founded, in this region, at Péc, the first metropolitan autocephaly (independent of the patriarch in Byzantium). With the birth of Yugoslavia in 1918, the two regions were united. National unity and the rediscovery of Serbian identity were successfully won through possession of two crucial places in the social imaginary.

For this reason, in the inter-war years, Yugoslavian governments, held largely by Serbians, tried an ambitious operation of ethnic re-balancing. In the inter-war years, Kosovo was the theater of an agrarian reform, which, cutting up the great possessions of the Ottoman era, gave new plots to poor Slavic-speaking farmers, who were forced to come from regions throughout the kingdom. Often, they were veterans of the war, quite willing to accept their new condition. But Albanian farmers would not benefit from the reforms, nor were they supposed to. Along with other vexations, and small and large impediments in life, agrarian reform was a strategic instrument designed to provoke Albanian emigration.

In 1937, Vasa Cubrilovic, who was considered by some Yugoslavians a hero for his participation in the 1914 Sarajevo assassination, presented a paper with the significant title of "The expulsion of the Albanians," in which he summarized possible strategies for achieving ethnic balance in Kosovo. To illustrate his arguments, Cubrilovic referred to a map in which the region annexed in 1878 carried the legend: "area cleansed of Albanians." He underlined with satisfaction expulsions that had occurred in the past and claimed the need to continue along those lines.

"Cleansing" pointed to the aspiration to reclaim an original state, the elimination of successive cultural stratifications, the elimination of traces of those events which in the eyes of Serbian nationalist were degradations of an original purity, deviations from the correct path of history. The connection between the Serbian nation and the entire territory seemed to Cubrilovic to be ancient, from the roots, and necessary. The Albanian population was considered temporary, linked to the equally transitory Ottoman domination. With the end of Ottoman dominion, Kosovo was once again in the hands of its legitimate owner, who would return to populate and govern it.

In the years between the wars, Yugoslavian authorities actually followed, at least in part, Cubrilovic's policies. Albanians were expelled, or sought refuge not just in their national state, but also in Turkey, appealing to its broader and more inclusive community of worship. On the basis of this criterion, in 1939–41, many Albanians found themselves in the middle of distant desert regions of Central Anatolia, which they had never populated, nor had any intention of populating.

The ideology of ethnic cleansing brought the Serbs to mystify their own historical origins. The arguments presented to make Kosovo Serbian, on the basis of natural right, because of the supposed greater antiquity of the population, could backfire. Serbians were certainly not the original inhabitants of the area. They were the descendants of those Slavic tribes who, during that great movement of peoples in the first centuries of our era, had abandoned their settlements between the Vistula and Dnepr (more or less between what today are Poland and Ukraine), to find a new home south of the Danube. The presence of the Albanians' ancestors in the Balkans, on the other hand, goes back much further.

Many mysteries envelop the origin and history of the Albanian language, recognized as such only in the fourteenth century. It contains many Slavic, Turkish, Greek, and Latin expressions. It is probable that it descended from Illyrian, a branch of the Indo-European peoples who, during the Roman Empire, had already settled in the Western Balkans (Istria, Dalmatia, Bosnia, Epirus, Albania itself) for many centuries, or millennia. Even if we have no evidence of the actual locations of the Albanian populations (or proto-Albanian, or late Illyrian) during the Middle Ages, there is no doubt that Albanians and Slavs (Serbians and Bulgarians) were strongly intertwined.

On the other hand, there is no certainty that the majority of the medieval, Albanian population was in the same region as today (Albania, Kosovo, Western Macedonia). According to many, they could have been located more to the North or West. In any case, there was close contact with Neo-Latin peoples, as the linguistic borrowings of today's Albanian attest. There has never been ethnic purity in any Balkan territory, nor has there ever been a static population. The call for purity and immutable roots is less than ever a cogent call for the future.

A few years after the annexation of Kosovo, a second front for expansion opened for Serbia, more ample and just as fraught with danger. After the victory of World War I, the expansion took a different form and direction. No longer east and south, towards territories that had for centuries belonged to the empire of the Ottoman Turks; but towards the west, and the north, towards territories that had belonged to the Habsburg Empire and the Republic of Venice. No longer in the form of a pure and simple territorial enlargement guaranteed by the division made by the great powers, but in the form of a free union between the Serbian kingdom, the Kingdom of Montenegro, and the various southern Slav people (Croats, Slovenians, Bosnians, and a not insignificant fraction of Serbians), who for centuries had belonged to the Habsburg Empire.

Almost 85% of the inhabitants of the new kingdom of the Serbs, Croats, and Slovenians were Slavic-speaking. If everything contributed to separating Serbians from Albanians (language, history, religion), a great deal of affinity seemed to link them to the peoples of the northern and western regions. In fact, the events of the previous century had left a heritage of a written and united language to more than 65% of the kingdom's population. But the religious and historic differences continued to be a great weight. In particular, Croats not only remained tied to the memory of a distant medieval kingdom, but had retained their own assembly (*Sabor*) through all the successive dominations, even when they had been reduced to a thin strip of land in the Habsburg Empire almost overwhelmed by Turkish pressure. In any case, those who had lived in the now defunct Austro-Hungarian Empire were used to regulations, procedures, and practices that were quite different from those of the kingdom of Serbia.

The prospect of a free union failed almost immediately when faced with the inability of the governments and above all the dynasties to confront, or even simply to perceive, the question of differences. On the contrary, a politics of deliberate fusion and assimilation of the Slav peoples in the kingdom took over, which, in fact, was based on a mechanical extension of the institutions of the old kingdom of Serbia. The Western peoples of the kingdom immediately perceived this as a direct threat to their identity. In a few months, from November 28, 1920 to June 28, 1921, the seeds were sown for the disastrous events of the immediate and distant future.

The 28th of November, date of the election for the kingdom's constitutive assembly, showed how deep the divisions and stratifications in the nation really were. All the assembly's parties, except for the Communists, had regional, religious, or ethno-linguistic roots. None enjoyed electoral favor throughout the entire territory. There were many good reasons to prefer a federal type of constitution, based on autonomy and the equilibrium of entities which corresponded to historical and national differences. Many proposals of this kind were presented to the assembly. But, in the end, precisely the opposite decision was taken, largely because of the main Serbian parties then in power.

The administrative division entailed by the Yugoslavian constitution was a direct imitation of the French system of departments and prefects. No consideration was made for the fact that the new state was born of the fusion of three antecedent states (Serbia, Montenegro, and Croatia, which for centuries had a separate existence), and of other territories annexed from Austria, Hungary, and Bulgaria. Not even the name of these antecedent identities was mentioned in the new territorial order, which was composed, instead, of 33 *oblasts*, small districts with little autonomy, which did not respect historical or natural borders. In 1929, this order was replaced by a new division into 9 large *banovinas*, strongly controlled by the center. From a symbolic perspective, this order was even worse than the preceding one. The banovinas had the names of rivers, almost to wipe out the names of the preceding entities, and their borders seemed conceived precisely to interrupt areas with relatively homogeneous identity. Kosovo, in particular, was divided among the banovinas of Morava (with the capital in Nis, in South-East Serbia), Vardar (with the capital in Skopje, in Macedonia), and Zeta (with the capital in Cetinje, in Montenegro). And in the official census, it was decided not to make any reference to distinct identities not only of Serbs, Croats, and Montenegrins, but also Macedonians, and Bulgarians, all included under the hybrid of "Serbo-Croats," which gave a distorted view of the make-up of the new state.

These choices were perceived as an affront by many of the new kingdom's constituents. Particularly strong was the resentment of the entire Croat nation, exacerbated by a bloody event. On the 20th of June 1928, during a session of the National Serbian Assembly (Skupstina), Punisa Racic, a deputy from Montenegro, close to the sovereign himself, mortally wounded Stjepan Radic, defender of the Croat national identity and party leader of the Farmers' party, which had either an absolute or a relative majority in almost all of Croatia. Over the years, the Croatian opposition became stronger and stronger, also because Mussolini's fascist government welcomed and protected the most extremist Croatian nationalists on Italian soil. In August of 1939, the fear of international complications was one of the main reasons which pushed the authoritarian regime in Belgrade to resuscitate the borders of the historical/ethnic entity of Croatia, creating a large autonomous banovina, which included the territories that had been divided by previous arrangements. But by now it was too late. The outbreak of World War II precipitated a series of events. The Nazi invasion of 1941 lead to the dismemberment of Yugoslavia and the takeover of the government of the satellite state of Croatia by fascist and ultra-nationalist *ustascia* (rebels), under the dictatorship of Ante Pavelic.

A terrible nemesis descended on the Serbian people. The Nazis assigned to their protectorate not only a great part of the banovina of 1939, but also the entire territory of Bosnia-Herzegovina and a fraction of Serbian territory, up to the gates of Belgrade. This greater Croatia was as multinational as the dissolved Yugoslavia, populated by Catholic Croats, Bosnian Muslims, Orthodox Serbs, and Jews. The *ustascia* government of Croatia accepted as citizens of its territory only Catholics and Muslims. As for the Orthodox Serbs and Jews, the chilling sentence was expressed with two key terms: "cleansing," and "purification." *Apartheid*, first of all: discriminations, religious persecutions, humiliations, matrimonial interdictions, the wearing of signs around the neck. Immediately after, the horrific "final solution:" a part of the Serbs would be expelled; another part, converted by force; and another would undoubtedly be eliminated. The program was followed with a phenomenal violence, which at times proved disconcerting to the Italian army, which acted as an ally and protector of the *ustascia*. The figures for the genocide are very controversial: 80,000 or 300,000 or a million Serbs massacred. In any case, they are substantial.

During World War II, ethnic cleansing went beyond the point of no return on the other side as well. The Chetniks, nationalist and ultranationalist Serbians, who fought both the Nazi invaders and Tito's Communist resistance, often trying a subtle game of balance between the two enemies, massacred Croatians and Bosnian Muslims. Theirs was not a simple reaction to the news of Croatian massacres: it was an autonomously theorized practice, designed to "cleanse" Serbian soil of "all non-Serbian elements."

Between *ustascia* and Chetniks there is no before and after. There is no causal reaction of action and reaction. On the contrary, it is the simultaneous and reciprocal crossing of a deadly threshold: the idolatry of the pure, or purified nation.

In the Yugoslavia of World War II, the ethnically-based massacres were intertwined with ideologically-based massacres. Internal ultranationalist fanaticism clashed with the two totalitarianisms of our century, and the Nazi and Stalinist totalitarianisms also clashed. It is a story of massacres by the invading Nazis and their allies against resistance of any sort (from the Chetniks to Tito's partisans). It is a story of nationalist and partisan reprisals against the invaders. It is a story which sometimes saw Chetniks massacre Communist partisans with the approval and the aid of the Nazis. It is a story in which Tito, almost at the end of the war, sacrificed many of his men for prestige, in an operation involving useless assaults against the occupying forces in full retreat. It is a story in which Communist partisans followed the soldiers and functionaries of Ante Pavelic, who were attempting to surrender to the English, to the village of Bleiburg between Slovenia and Austria: they imprisoned a large part of them, and brutally massacred almost all of them (around 20,000 or 30,000 persons). Tito prided himself that he had done some good house *cleaning*.

In this story, nobody is innocent. Of this story nobody can say, in the Balkans or anywhere in Europe, what the German Emperor told his soldiers during World War I: "this is not what I wanted."

Today, when the second Yugoslavia, which existed from 1945 to 1992, has tragically ended in blood in ways that are very reminiscent of the end of the first Yugoslavia, we discover the ambivalence surrounding this inconvenient and deeply rooted past. For a moment, the victory of Tito's army of liberation and the rapid Soviet influence seemed to point to the possibility of overcoming inter-ethnic conflicts. In particular, after 1945, Yugoslavia, Albania, and Bulgaria found themselves governed by ruling classes which had fought the same invaders side by side, brought together by the same ideology. For a short time, a larger Balkan federation seemed conceivable, including Albania and Bulgaria: perhaps this federation would have permitted the old questions of Kosovo and Macedonia on a new and de-dramatized basis. In the very first few years after World War II, many leaders of the national Communist parties operated in this direction. The clashes within the dominant élites, but above all Moscow's divide and rule policy, eliminated this project's possibility. In 1949, after Tito's break with Stalin, and Bulgaria and Albania's alignment with the Moscow bloc, the Balkan federation ended up with all the other unrealized ideas. The Albanian and Macedonian questions became an uncomfortable inheritance for the new Yugoslavian leadership, which already had to use all its imagination to heal the wound the massacres of *ustasci* and Chetniks had created in the country.

To de-dramatize both fronts which had remained critical for the identity of the country (the southern one inherited from 1913, the eastern one inherited from 1918), Tito and the new ruling class devised an innovative institutional form, which was intended to take off from the 1939 reform and was to generalize it throughout the territory. The new republic was to be federal and its subdivisions would return to mirroring the ethnic and historical identities of the country. The six resulting entitites would reflect the six nations (*narod*) of the southern Slavs (*Juznosloven*) who inhabited the soil of the republic, which history had given a distinct identity.

The territory of Slovenia, very ethnically compact, was easily defined. For Montenegro, the borders of 1914 were followed, but with exceptions: in fact, it obtained the Bay of Kotor, of great strategic relevance, which in the past had been a part of the Habsburg territories. More problematic was the distinction between the territories of the Serb, Croatian, and Muslim nations, in many areas inextricably interconnected. The solution consisted in reviving the historical entity of Bosnia-Herzegovina annexed by Austria in 1878, distinct inasmuch as it was both territory of the new Croatia (largely obtained from Hungary until 1918, and to a lesser extent coinciding with Dalmatia, which was first Venetian and then Habsburgian), and of Serbia, centered on the new kingdom. Macedonia, finally, obtained as a border what had been the line of separation between Serbia and the Ottoman Empire from 1878 until 1912. And, above all, a Macedonian language was recognized, distinct both from Serbian and Bulgarian, to be promoted with education and the establishment of precise written rules.

Similar strategies were put into act in order to dedramatize the equally thorny problem of the other Yugoslavian (*Jugosloven*) nationalities (*narodnosti*): those ethnic minorities which had a nation-state beyond the borders of Yugoslavia and had hopes of being reunited. In 1913, the Ottoman defeat left Serbia and Montenegro an inheritance of hundreds of thousands of Albanians. In 1920, the treaty of Trianon left the Yugoslavians an inheritance of many hundreds of thousands of Hungarians. In the re-apportionment of the republics after World War II, much of the area with Albanian and Hungarian populations were again brought within the borders of the new Serbia. For both these areas, the hybrid status of "autonomous province" was created: while still belonging (in the larger context of the Yugoslavian federation) to the Serbian Republic, both areas were endowed with considerable possibilities for self-government. With the constitution of 1974, this autonomy was strengthened even more: Kosovo and Vojvdina (an ancient name that was resuscitated to define the region with many ethnicities immediately north of Belgrade, at the confluence of the Danube, Tisa, and the Sava) practically became new republics, even if undeclared, of the federation.

But the peculiar balance between the two republics, two autonomous provinces, and many nations and nationalities, began to fall apart at the very moment that it was put together.

In the sixties, the last decade of Tito's long regime, the internal life of Yugoslavia was characterized by three conflicts of interests and perspectives that interacted and complicated each other: the Communist reformers ("liberals") pitted against the dogmatic conservatives; the rich northwestern republics (Slovenia and Croatia) pitted against the poorer republics; finally, centralizing Serbia against all the other decentralizing republics. The mosaic of opinions became extremely complicated. The temptation to simplify it with cleansings of the ruling classes became perilously frequent.

It was precisely on the ancient southern front, in Kosovo, that the instabilities went beyond the point of no return. Many Serbian leaders and intellectuals, were hiding their faith in the ultranationalist ideology of the first half of the century behind a ritual and extremely thin veneer of Communist ideology. For them, the constitution of 1974 was a threat to the territorial integrity of the Serbian state, but above all an insult to the collective imagination of the Serbian nation. For the Communist leaders and the Albanian intellectuals of Kosovo, the question appeared in exactly the opposite light: Tito's concessions and the new Yugoslavian constitution had stopped just short of being irreversible. Only the official status of a federal republic would have satisfied the claims of the Albanian nationals. This was the call to arms for the risings which exploded in 1981, and with which the Albanians protested the return of repressive politics to Belgrade. The clashes ended with heavy tribunal sentences, and above all with the dismantling of the Yugoslavian constitution itself. Kosovo was for all intents and purposes demoted to the role of ordinary Yugoslavian province, with little or no autonomy in decision-making.

In 1986, the Serbian intellectuals of the prestigious Academy of Arts and Sciences, with the support of an emerging new political class, asserted in a memorandum that this was still too much, that the concession of self-government to the Albanians had been a dangerous concession, that the Albanian demographic development would threatened Serbs' very identity, that the Serbs had undoubtedly been victims of the Croatians and Slovenians, that the constitution of 1974 should be abolished forthwith....

On the 28th of June 1989, a million people gathered in the heart of Kosovo, in the plains where six hundred years earlier the Serbian people had fought its heroic battle against the Ottomans. Slobodan Milosevic, President of the Communist League of Serbia, wanted to revive the "reconquest of Kosovo," and the "reunification of the whole of Serbia." Behind the rhetoric, the expressions were hiding the will to destroy the political, cultural, and economic rights of the Albanian ethnicity, the will to suppress the autonomy and the self-government of the autonomous province of Kosovo, and, in the end, the will to bury the Yugoslavian constitution of 1974.

From 1986 to 1989, Milosevic had strenuously pursued this objective, organizing mass rallies to marshal the resentment of Serbs and Montenegrins who lived in Kosovo, promising "law and order," making great cleansings in the ranks of the Serbian Communist Party itself, and also normalizing the governments of Vojvodina and Montenegro. The Albanians once more battled for their rights, which had been attacked along with the constitution. In March of 1989, the army responded harshly: 24 people were killed, and 44 arrested: all of Albanian ethnicity. Immediately afterward, Kosovo and Vojvodina were forced to vote for their disappearance as autonomous entities. Milosevic and his group blamed the events on the "chauvinism " and "separatism" of the Albanians.

Within the Albanian federation, the repression of Kosovo had very serious repercussions. In the Eastern republics (Slovenia and Croatia), it was understood as a threshold which made impossible any reform of or agreement with the federation or the Serbian republic's ruling class. It was perceived as an invitation to secession.

Edgar Morin has lucidly described the final European tragedy of a tragic century, coining the enlightening term total-nationalism. Ethnic cleansing, an idea which throughout our century has brought death and ruin, has been resuscitated by an incompetent sorcerer's apprentice, by a restricted totalitarian *élite*, which was suddenly without the legitimation of the ancient Communist ideology, and sought desperately for a ready-to-use secondary ideology.

Out of control, the demon erupted among those nearest the epicenter. It swept up the Serbs in its wake: now removed from the process with which Europe seeks unification; now plagued by one of the worst inflations of their economic history and who are now beginning to leave, now that the web of both intra- and inter- ethnic solidarity, which fed their cultures, has unraveled....

The tragic irony of fate has ensured that the principal scapegoats should be those Serbo-Croat-speaking Bosnian Muslims who had managed to survive the other crises relatively unharmed: the crisis of the first, centralist and authoritarian Yugoslavia of World War II, and the second, Communist and federal Yugoslavia. But the Bosnian Muslims had been in the sights of ethnic cleansing for quite some time.

Bosnia, like Kosovo, was also a part of the Serbs' national plans at the end of the last century and at the beginning of this one. In Bosnia, as in Kosovo, the nationalists wanted a return to the original conditions. In their eyes, the Bosnian Muslims were nothing but Serbs who had become Turkish, who in the centuries of Ottoman domination had renounced their nation's only faith: they should be brought back to the faith of their fathers. In 1917, Stojan Protic, who was to become president of the council of the new kingdom of Serbs, Croats and Slovenians, formulated "re-conversion," his solution for Bosnia after the war: "When our Army crosses the Drina, it will give the Turks 24 or 48 hours to return to the faith of the ancestors. Whoever refuses, will be massacred, as we have massacred in Serbia."

Protic had evoked the tragedy which, beyond the Drina, was accomplished 75 years later. The historical tornado hesitated for a long time before returning to Sarajevo. But the announced tragedy was preceded by many other tragedies, and nobody stopped the infernal chain of events. In the meantime, a further step towards the abyss was made, when compared to Protic's formulation, a further barbarism. From the project of homogenization of the other, we have moved to the stark unwillingness to accept the other. Beyond the Drina, today, nobody is trying to convert anybody. It is not a question of religion any more, there isn't even the escape route of dropping an ancient identity and assuming a new general identity. The "other" remains inevitably "other." Alterity is an indelible mark. The choices are restricted: escaping, being chased out, or being killed. When the time and space for escape are missing, when the winner brings the obsession of purification to the depths of the abyss, the choices are reduced to the extreme.

# 13

## Eastern Central Europe today

### Between forced normalization and ideas of association

In a period of 180 years, between 1815 and 1994, the picture of Eastern Central Europe has been turned completely upside down. The great multi-national empires (Austria, Russia, and the Ottoman Empire), disturbed, metamorphosed, and disintegrated by an interminable series of wars and internal conflicts, have been replaced by almost entirely mono-ethnic republics (Austria and Germany), or with a strong national majority (Turkey and Russia). In comparison with the geographical space that was the domain of the multi-national empires, the new republics are smaller and with a new center of gravity: Austria and Germany have become an integral part of Western Central Europe; Turkey has the majority of its territory in Asia; the double collapse of the Czarist and Soviet empires has deprived Russia of all the parts of its dominion in proximity to Central Europe.

In the intermediate space, in the Eastern Central Europe which today's geopolitics tends to define as the middle of Europe, the events of the last two centuries have created many small and medium-sized states, all characterized by the presence of an ethnic majority, and all tormented by many issues regarding the drawing of borders and the rights of ethnic minorities.

In 1815, there were no independent nation-states alongside the great multi-national empires in Eastern Central Europe.

In 1914, after the spectacular retreat of the Ottoman Empire, the region's nation-states were seven, including Hungary, which considered itself a full state, even though it was a part of the Habsburg Empire.

In 1920, after the almost simultaneous collapse of the four empires (Czarist, Habsburg, German, and Ottoman), the states had risen to twelve, and they remained so until 1938.

The division of Eastern Central Europe between Hitler and Stalin, and the Second World War, saw the suppression of many independent states, and, on the other hand, many ephemeral independencies.

In 1945, the post-war order fixed 9 nation-states in the region, and so they remained until 1990, the year of the Warsaw Pact countries' democratic transition and of German Unification.

In the short span of three years, the break-up of Yugoslavia, the dissolution of the Soviet Union, the consensual divorce between Czechs and Slovaks, have lead to twenty nation-states in the region. Indeed, their number rises to 23 if we consider the states of the southern Caucasus (Georgia, Armenia, Azerbaijan), which have shared much of the history of Eastern Central Europe: the border condition between Russia and Turkey, the Ottoman dominion and the Czarist dominion, the wars of 1878 and 1914, the break-up of the Czarist empire, the uncertain period of wars and peace treaties following World War I, the construction of the new Soviet Empire, the dissolution of this Second Empire....

The history of the formation of the nation-states of Eastern Central Europe is a history of singular events, sometimes divergent, sometimes convergent, at times, in clear opposition.... It is the story not only of the liberation of peoples and proclamations of independence, but also of radical institutional changes, foreign invasions, annihilations of state entities, border disputes, arbitrarily resettled populations, spectacular shifts in allegiance, enemies who become friends and friends who become enemies, oppressors who become oppressed, and oppressed who become oppressors.

From the interweavings of this tormented story there emerge, nevertheless, some interesting constants:

1. Even if single events are heterogeneous and, at times, contradictory, their concatenation has outlined an uninterrupted process, during the course of which an entire area has redesigned itself along ethnic-national borders, or at least what are perceived to be such. This process, already in movement in the first half of the 19th century with the decline of the Ottoman Empire, has seen moments of dramatic acceleration, coinciding with an increase in armed conflicts (1877–78; 1912–22; 1938–45), and moments in which the *status quo* was frozen (1923–28; 1945–90), which nevertheless did nothing to change the territory being contested.

2. In Eastern Central Europe of the last two centuries, not only have ancient empires collapsed, but new ones have been created: the Soviet Union (1922–91) and Hitler's third *Reich* (1933–45). Compared to the tendency for

the affirmation of local national identities, their expansionist attempts have, in a certain sense, been a counter-current. Soviet foreign policy, in fact, gave itself as an objective the continuation and completion of the Russian march towards the West. Hitlerism brought to a fever pitch and absolutized the multi-century *Drang Nach Osten* of the German people toward the Slavic peoples. The Second World War in Eastern Central Europe saw not only the clash of national tendencies and imperialist counter-tendencies, but also saw the clash of two imperial counter-tendencies (German and Russian). The dramatic nature of these clashes is shown by the swift elimination from the map of 7 states (Czechoslovakia, Albania, Poland, Estonia, Lithuania, Latvia, Yugoslavia), in only two years (1939–1941).

3. The present acceleration is the most intense to date in terms of immediate effects, when compared to the previous ones. It has almost been an explosion: if at the beginning of 1990 there were 9 independent states in the spaces between Germany, Austria, Russia, and Turkey, today, only 4 years later, there are 20 (or 23), more than double. On the other hand, from another perspective, this acceleration has also been the completion of a process. All the major ethnicities in this part of Europe have become the nucleus of a nation-state, and, vice versa, all the nation-states have a dominant ethnicity as a nucleus. There are only a few exceptions. Romania and Moldavia have the same ethnicity as a nucleus, and their division is due more than anything to political opportunity. The "third" Yugoslavia, on the other hand, continues to associate Serbs and Montenegrins, who in many ways consider themselves as belonging to different ethnicities (even if the basis of their differentiation is not linguistic or religious, but purely historical). Bosnia-Herzegovina remains the one truly multi-ethnic state in the region, and it is precisely in this state that multi-ethnic coexistence has been tested most severely.

4. The separation of ethnicities through new national borders, characteristic of the last four years, does not guarantee stability at all. On the contrary, the secession of ethnic minorities from the new states is extremely frequent. In the last years, we have seen the secession of Serbs in Croatia, Serbs in Bosnia, Croats in Bosnia, Muslims in the region of Bihac in Bosnia itself, Russians in Moldavia, Christian Turks in Moldavia, Abkhazians in Georgia, Ossetians in Georgia, Armenians in Azerbaijan.... Complicating matters are the *enclaves*, possessions of a state which do not form a part of the main body of the state itself, leftovers from previous geopolitical orders. Eastern Prussia (the province of Kaliningrad) belongs to the Russian Federation, but

is isolated between Poland and Lithuania and separated from the body of
Russia by the presence of Lithuania and Byelorussia. Nahicevan belongs to
Azerbaijan, but is surrounded by Turkey, Iran, and Armenia: it is the latter
which separates it from the main body of its state.

5. In the last century, almost every state has experienced changes of
borders, and real shifts in center of gravity. Many regions, conversely, have
changed allegiance several  times (the region of Vilnius between Lithuania
and eastern Poland, Macedonia, Thrace, Southern Dobrogea). But despite all
the new orders, and the dismantling of these new orders, the coincidence
between national borders and ethnic borders (linguistic, religious) was (and
is) always imperfect and the source of interminable conflict. Almost every
state contained (and contains) in its territory many ethnic minorities.
Conversely, many ethnicities have found themselves (and are finding
themselves) separated in several chunks by the new borders, and in the
difficult and ambiguous situation of being the majority in one and the
minority in another. Particularly problematic, in the long run, is the situation
of what used to be the dominant ethnicities of the multi-national empires
which in the past divided up these parts of Europe between themselves. The
German and Turkish presence  is almost completely gone. Today the
Russian presence, massive in almost all the republics of the ex-Soviet Union,
is the source of new conflicts.

6. The precariousness of borders and the complexity of the population are
two causes for the congenital weakness of the new states' identity. This
identity has to be continuously reinvented, on the basis of old and new
historical, geographical, ethnic, cultural, and spiritual narratives, at times
mutually incompatible. Faced with such congenital weakness, the ruling
classes of the new states have tried to make their states achieve an identity
comparable to that of the Western Central European states through a set of
forced stages.  For this purpose, a strategy of fusion has been adopted: the
attempt to neutralize and almost forget linguistic, cultural, and spiritual
particular-ities of the individual components of a nation, in order to achieve
a high degree of homogeneity on which to found the new concept of
citizenship. In reality, this has lead to a mechanical adoption, a crystalliza-
tion, an impoverishment of the ideas and practices which Eastern Central
Europe had created in the preceding centuries. A second strategy was the
separation of ethnicities through the raising of symbolic borders, such as the
failure to provide certain cultural or political rights to some collectivities, or
through the pure and simple expulsion of the undesired ethnicities. "Ethnic

cleansing" in the horrifying sense in which we are witnessing it, can be considered a degenerate (albeit frighteningly consistent) and extreme form of the latter strategy.

From the point of view of the ethnic population, the nation-states of Central Eastern Europe today are characterized by recent and, at times, arbitrary borders. The footsteps and stratifications of history reappear in the population of many areas.

Vojvodina and Banat are two regions on the left bank of the middle part of the Danube, between the Pannonian plane and the Transylvanian Alps. Both became Habsburg possessions in the first half of the 18th century, when the Ottoman Empire began to recede. After 1867, they belonged to the Hungarian part of the empire. In 1920, the Treaty of Trianon detached the two regions from the new nation-state of Hungary, giving a large part to Yugoslavia and the eastern part of Banat to Rumania. As we have seen, after the war Vojvodina became an autonomous province of the Federal Serb Republic, which it remains to this day. The regions show, above all, fringes of interference between adjacent nationalities. Many areas of Serbian Vojvodina contain large Hungarian minorities and even majorities. Furthermore, there are Rumanian enclaves in Serbian Vojvodina, Hungarian enclaves in Rumanian Banat, and Serbian enclaves in southern Hungary, near the border.

When they were annexed, the regions constituted the marker which the Habsburg Empire developed in the 18th century along the eastern part of the Ottoman border with the Balkans, from the Adriatic to Transylvania. In those days, the area was completely depopulated and devastated, following emigrations due to the Turkish expansion and the wars to reconquer lost territory. In the second half of the 18th century, the Habsburg emperors' policy was to call farmers from all regions of the empire, including extreme regions, and to give them settlements, land, and, above all, freedom from feudal constraints, in exchange for two duties: agricultural colonization and border patrols. In this way, Slovaks, Ukrainians, Bulgarians, Czechs, and Germans, to mention only a few of the nationalities that survive to this day, came to settle in the region side by side, village by village. The regions obviously show the imprint of events after 1920. The minorities of the new nation-states became less important without disappearing completely. One ethnicity, nevertheless, almost completely disappeared from Vojvodina and Yugoslavian Banat: Germans, expelled at the end of the Second World War because of the collaboration of many with the Nazi invaders.

Immediately to the North of Banat, is the border between Hungary and
Rumania—also fixed in 1920 with the Treaty of Trianon. We have seen that
this border was drawn not only for purely ethnic considerations but also for
strategic purposes: favoring the Rumanians and not the Hungarians. It is no
surprise, therefore, that in the Rumanian districts of the plains there are still
significant Hungarian minorities: 38% in the Satu-Mare district, 31% in the
Bihor district, and so forth. Hungarians are not in the majority in any of the
border areas, but they have substantial majorities that are quite distant from
borders, in Transylvania, by the eastern Carpathians: in the district of
Harghita (around 84%) and the district of Covasna (around 78%). The
Hungarians are descendants of an ancient ethnicity, the so-called *Széklers*.
They speak the same language and belong to the same cultural community as
the Magyars of the Pannonian plain, but, in part, have different origins.
According to some, the *Széklers* accompanied the Avars in their terrifying
invasions, preceding the Magyars themselves by a few centuries. Others
claim they were a Turkic tribe (Khazars) which adopted the Magyar
language.

Finally, a fourth ethnic group has settled in those places since remote
times. These are Saxons—Germans who came from the Rheinland in 1150,
and contributed to the rebirth of Transylvania after the disastrous Mongol
invasions of 1241–1242.

The history of the Hungarians and Rumanians of Transylvania, and the
story of their relations, is particularly controversial. While the Hungarian
settlement dates to around the time of their descent into the Pannonian
plain—from the ninth to tenth centuries—the origin and history of the
Rumanians has lead to two different hypotheses. The first hypothesis considers the Rumanians of Transylvania direct descendants of the ancient
Dacians, who were Latinized in the second Century CE. Although tormented
by successive invasions (Goths, Gepids, Avars, Slavs, Pechenegs), they were
not destroyed by them. On the contrary, the hypothesis is that the invaders
were assimilated. In any case, their settlement preceded the Magyars and the
*Széklers* in the region. According to the second hypothesis, the nucleus of
the Rumanian ethnicity located itself in a totally different place: a triangle of
Nis-Skopje-Sofia, centered more or less around what today is Macedonia.
Following this hypothesis, the Wallachians still present in this area (Albania,
Serbia, Greece) are not Rumanians who left their lands. It is the Rumanians
who left other nuclei of the same branch, following the reverse route. They
reached the Bulgarian banks of the Danube and then, around the 8th century,

went beyond it reaching Wallachia and Transylvania. In that age, Magyars and *Széklers* had already been in those places for centuries. Even though this question is far from settled, "neutral" scholars generally consider the latter hypothesis more plausible.

But this is not a purely academic dispute. Even in the apparently "internationalist" decades of "real" socialism, the Rumanian authorities stood firmly behind the first hypothesis, while the Hungarians supported the second. The Ceausescu regime in particular more than once referred to the Hungarian historians, who denied the thesis of a continuous Rumanian population in Transylvania as revisionists or fascists. This degree of vitriol can be explained by the fact that in play is the same way of thinking which we saw in action, with such destructive results, in the conflict of words and facts between Serbs and Albanians concerning Kosovo. Whoever can claim to have arrived somewhere first can claim a historic right to the territory regardless of further historical events. In such a case, in areas of continuous exchange and ethnic stratification, the past is "cleansed" to defend one's identity (or to attack somebody else's).

East of Hungary and Rumania, the band of six republics that in 1991 obtained their independence from the Soviet Union (Estonia, Latvia, Lithuania, Byelorussia, Ukraine, and Moldavia) contains many of the ethnic and linguistic dynamics, which characterize the whole of Europe.

We can find there fringes of interference and superimposition between bordering ethnic groups (between Poland and Byelorussia, between Byelorussia and Ukraine); linguistic "islands" (Greeks who for centuries have settled on the coast of the Black Sea; Bulgarians and Hungarians in some areas of Ukraine; and even Jewish and Islamic Tartars who still live in Lithuania); areas with a very high linguistic and ethnic complexity (the region of Vilnius in Lithuania, populated by Poles, Lithuanians, Byelorussians, and Russians); small nationless ethnic minorities (Christian Turks of Moldavia). We can also find a state with a problematic identity, such as Moldavia, whose actual relations with Rumania are very reminiscent of the relations between Austria and Germany from 1918 (or 1866) to this day: an ethno-linguistic community divided in two by the events of history.

The region's main ethnic problem is a different one. It arises from the presence, in all six republics, of Russian-speaking individuals with Russian culture. In many areas, the nucleus of the Russian presence dates back to the period of Czarist expansion (1700–1900). In others, the decisive impulse occurred after the end of World War II. In some areas, the Russian element is concentrated in particular around the borders with the Russian federation (Eastern Ukraine, Eastern Estonia). In other areas, the Russian element is nevertheless concentrated territorially, as in the small area of Moldavia on the left bank of the Dnestr, and it is precisely the compact nature of the population that allowed the Russians, after 1991, to bring up the possible specter of secession.

But apart from these localized cases, in the totality of the republics, large clusters of Russians are spread throughout the territory. Generally, the urban and industrialized areas have a much higher number of Russians than the rural ones. This situation has provoked strong tensions—particularly in Estonia and Latvia. The two local ethnicities, whose relation to the Russian ethnicity in the years before independence (1920–1939) was respectively between 10:1 and 6:1, today have seen their numbers reduced: in 1989, in Estonia the ratio of Estonians to Russians was around 2 to 1, while in Latvia the ratio of Latvians to Russians has gone down to a little above 1.5 to 1. In any case, in the Baltic states, Russians have become the overwhelming majority in some cities and neighborhoods.

The omnipresence of the Russian ethnic group, the frequent and, at times, spasmodic change of borders in the years from the October revolution and the two World Wars, and the more ancient ethnic and linguistic tensions, are three factors that, together, make the national identity of the former Soviet republics even more threatened and, at least, weaker than that of other Central European states. The range of problems for the new states is enormous: difficulties in the recovery and generalization of little used languages which were almost clandestine during Czarist and Soviet years (as is the case in Ukraine and Byelorussia); identities threatened by the Russian presence which, in turn react with relatively intolerant acts (Estonia, Latvia); an artificial identity created by the expansion of the Soviet empire, leading to questions today about the reasons for its own survival or dissolution (Moldavia). Of all these states, Lithuania is perhaps the one with the most stable identity, both on an ethnic and a historical level.

For the states immediately to the West of the border which, until 1991, marked the limits of the Soviet Union, in what geographers call Middle Europe, there is another threat: forced normalization.

Today, the ethnic structure of the states in this region has become more homogenous than it was immediately after World War I. In 1920, the Middle-European states were explicitly multi-national (Yugoslavia and Czechoslovakia), or, along with a definite majority, were hosts to many ethnic minorities (23 minorities in Rumania, for instance). Among these minorities, present everywhere, were the Jews, especially in Poland (7.8% of the total population).

Today, Czechoslovakia has disappeared, leaving in its place one generally mono-national state (Slovenia) and four states where the relation between majorities and minorities are the cause of conflict or open warfare. In the states which already in 1920 had a clearly defined ethnic majority, the proportion between majority and minority has generally changed in favor of the latter: Poles were 69.2% of the population of Poland in 1921, and 97% in 1991; Rumanians were 70.8% of the population of Rumania in 1930, and 89.4% in 1992.... Together with the Jews, other groups which had been rooted for centuries (Saxons in Transylvania, Wallachians in Greece and Serbia) are almost completely disappearing from the regions they populated.

The comparison with the relative ethnic homogeneity of many countries in Western Central Europe is, in many respects, misleading. In the West, the relative ethnic homogeneity of the population is the result of many centuries of history. This history has certainly been marked by violence and abuse— particularly against rural populations and religious non-conformists. But it is a history where an important role has also been played by processes of convergence, fusion, collective education, and the construction of civil society and citizenship. In Eastern Central Europe, on the other hand, we see the almost immediate rupture of a space which has always been multi-ethnic, and which has drawn precisely from this multi-ethnicity many of the distinctive characteristics of its identity. This sudden discontinuity has allowed and favored a generalized revolt against memories, a rationalization and rewriting of history which reflects only the reasons of the winners. But not all the memories have disappeared, and not all memories allow themselves to be erased easily.

We therefore have to ask ourselves a more disquieting question: is this order—even if very simplified and impoverished (the result of endless killing and unspeakable suffering)—viable today? Is this the price to be paid so that a new history can begin, capable of leading the people of Central Eastern Europe into a new, Western European context? Events in not only the former Yugoslavia, but also Georgia (a region similar in many respects), suggest we should not be too confident. In Yugoslavia, as in Georgia, inter- and intra-ethnic solidarities are collapsing, and an implosion towards the local is accelerating, with the risk that it will carry on forever.

In the Balkans, 1993 was not only the year of a tripolar total war, of all against all, between Serbs, Croats, and Bosnian Muslims. It was also the year in which Moslems opposed other Moslems—in the region of Bihac, the extreme northern corner of Bosnia. It was the year in which Montenegro, on its knees because of hyperinflation and the wartime economy, showed its secessionist tendencies in the small Yugoslavia, which still links it to Serbia. It was the year in which Istria, concerned about the hardening of nationalism in the Croatian government, has sought a way out in a new regional identity. It was the year in which the truce in Kosovo, Sanjak, and in Macedonia remained very precarious. And in Georgia, we see both the revolt of minorities (Abkhazians and Ossetians) against a new majority, considered oppressive (the Georgians), and the detachment of entire regions of the country, which became almost like personal fiefdoms of local warlords. In the former Yugoslavia, as in Georgia, the regression has swiftly retraced the steps of history, towards a situation similar to that of a thousand years ago, when—in large portions of the European territory—no state authority accompanied and governed the local powers. But the race towards pre-modernity risks going hand in hand with a horrible post-modernity, with the planetary traffic of the various mafias and drug-smugglers, who know well how to profit from the free zones.

But even without addressing the possibility of a disintegration, which in the long-term risks becoming irreversible, the experience of Central-Eastern Europe in the last 100 years has clearly shown that the exchange of popula-tions and the attempt to make the territories of the nation-states more homogenous no matter what it takes, is certainly not a valid way of avoiding conflicts. On the contrary, it is often the cause of conflicts. The connection individuals, collectivities, and ethnic groups have with a territory which they were forced to leave does not decrease over time and space. On the contrary, this connection can intensify, and settle in the deepest layers of the psyche, and sooner or later become an aggressive nationalism. The connection of the Serbian people with the land of Kosovo has not diminished despite the fact that Serbs have had their main centers of population in more northern regions. Every event of its history used to, and still does, raise issues of political domination, and in the more extreme cases of mass ethnic resettlement. The events following 1981 were just the last link in a long chain.

In the last few centuries of Europe's history, the simplifications imposed by winners during the rewriting of history has perpetuated a feud without end, in which the winner literally sows the seeds for future defeats. The events in the Balkans today are no exception. Let us think of the feud between the French and the Germans, which today seems very remote, for "fair" and "natural" borders, the continuously alternating sovereignty of Alsace-Lorraine, the crystallizations which lead to talk of "hereditary enemies," the millions who died in Verdun and the Marne. Western Europe in 1945, destroyed and annihilated, has left an important contribution to the forms of co-existence, creating a loosening of borders and national tensions, which deserves to be continued and meditated upon. Precisely because of this, what occurs in Bosnia-Herzegovina does not speak of a small corner of the world. It speaks of our recent history, of a Europe oscillating between abysses of cruelty and the realization of civilization.

Central Eastern Europe today requires a loosening of borders (rather than their abolition) analogous to the one which occurred at the end of the Second World War in Western Europe. In the years following 1989, a rich discussion has taken place among the states and areas of Europe in an effort to find new ways of coexistence among peoples and nations. This dialogue has been submerged and obscured by the barbaric abyss in which Sarajevo and its surroundings have collapsed. But it has not been interrupted. Today, against the reappearance of ethnic tribalisms, it may appear to be a weak dialogue, a counter-tendency fighting a more violent tendency. But the dialogue is not in vain. Decades ago, in Western Europe the voices for partnership were likewise in the minority. And for Western Europe today, still exposed to the risk of fragmentation, thinking about how its own experience can assist the path of other areas of the continent is by no means an idle pastime.

In the first place, in many states in Central Eastern Europe the minorities have come out into the open, claiming their rights and their very existence. The new political pluralism is often an important means to guarantee ethnic pluralism. In Bulgaria, the party which represents citizens of Turkish origin, or, more generally, of Islamic faith, has obtained a strong parliamentary representation, and has become decisive for the composition of the government. The Germans and Byelorussians of Poland have also had access, thanks to the constitution of that country, to their autonomous representation in parliament.

In the second place, Central Eastern Europe is also encountering problems of regional identity, of institutional reforms, of administrative decentralization. Ukraine, where the ethnic question due to the presence of millions of Russians is accompanied by a considerable regional diversification, is taking into consideration the possibility of adopting certain principles of the German constitution. The country would be divided into 16 autonomous units, many of which appear as expressions of ancient ethnic identities: Galicia, Bukovina, Donets Basin, Volhynia....

In the third place, Eastern Central Europe is a promising area for trans-border cooperation projects. In the last decades, in Western Europe, particularly within the twelve countries of the European Community, the borders have been crossed by a thick web of associations and connections, ranging from tourism to the economic to the cultural and ecological. At times, the border becomes a real attractor, which has multiplied the flux of individuals and ideas on both sides of the border, among centers and nearby regions. At times, the trans-border cooperation has lead to the forgetting of ethnic and national conflicts: between Germany and France in the case of Alsace, between Italy and Austria in the case of the Tyrol, and so forth. Starting in 1990, a project has been started to create areas of trans-border cooperation along the entire border between Germany and Poland and the next border between Germany and the Czech Republic. From the Baltic to Bavaria, seven "Euro-regions" have been identified with the purpose of reuniting territories which have been particularly hard hit by the borders and forced migrations of our century. Beyond any cultural and symbolic value, the Euro-regions have an important economic aspect: they have been developed as outposts of the European Economic Community towards the East, through which countries of Eastern Central Europe can be financed for specific projects.

In the fourth place, the states of Eastern Central Europe have shown the need for cooperation within the great regional wholes which were conceived of as a way of overcoming the ancient borders between blocks and types of economies. In 1992, two of these wholes were institutionalized: The Baltic Council and the Economic Community of the Black Sea. The first includes ten countries: Norway, Sweden, Finland, Russia, Estonia, Latvia, Lithuania, Poland, Germany, and Denmark. The second includes eleven countries: Albania, Greece, Turkey, Bulgaria, Rumania, Moldavia, Ukraine, Russia, Armenia, Georgia, and Azerbaijan. Both areas are marked by ethnic tensions and economic inequity. Both associations include countries in search of economic help, investments, and technical assistance. Both associations include countries in search of new markets. Will economic cooperation succeed in triggering a loosening of borders, as it did in Western Europe after the Second World War?

# 14

## From the Bosphorus to the Caspian Sea

### Two hinge-spaces between Europe and Asia

Turkey, the states of the Caucasus (Georgia, Armenia, Azerbaijan) and the Russian Federation are states we can define as Eurasian. These states define particularly interesting ethnic spaces. In these spaces, the effects of ancient migrations, of modern imperial migrations, emerging nationalities and linguistic and national constructs are comparable to those of Europe proper, but are at times also very divergent and peculiar.

The Turkish Republic can be defined as Eurasian first of all because of geographic reasons. After the first World War, and the collapse of the Ottomans, Turkey has retained, on European soil, Eastern Thrace and Istanbul (which spills over onto Asian soil). Regarding its surface, it is little more than 3% of the entire Turkish Republic. But, it counts for 10.5% of the population.

Turkey can be defined as a hinge-space between Europe and Asia for reasons which involve history and politics, the past and the present.

Turkish governments, since the end of the last war, have acted in such a way as to ensure the recognition of their country as a European state *tout court*. A member of the EC, a member of NATO since 1952, associate of the EC since 1963, Turkey has emphasized its willingness to be integrated into Europe's process of political and economic unification with an official request to join the EC presented in 1987. Today, it is one of the principal movers in an area of regional cooperation forming around the Economic Community of the Black Sea. Turkey is also actively involved in the construction of infrastructural axes (railways, fiber optics) Italy-Albania-Macedonia, Bulgaria-Turkey. Finally, important in Europe's contemporary imaginary, Turkey participates in the European sports world, particularly in the principal European team sport cups such as soccer, basketball, and volleyball.

From the present, let us move back to the past, to remember that today's Turkish state, (Eastern Thrace, Anatolia, the southern coast of the Black Sea, Taurus Mountains, High Mesopotamia) was from A.D. 395 to 1918 the central nucleus of two multi-national empires, whose history was linked to that of the entire Balkan peninsula and whose influence on Europe has at times been even greater (the Byzantine Empire reached southern Italy; the Ottoman Empire reached Hungary). The memories and the identities of the peoples of South-Eastern Europe have been irreversibly marked by the development of this multi-ethnic and multi-cultural space, which the present borders between nation-states have restructured, but not interrupted.

A common destiny brings together today's Turkey and the various Balkan nations (Greece, Bulgaria, Rumania, Albania, Macedonia, Serbia, Montenegro...) which were first subject to, then rebelled against, Ottoman domination. Like these states, Turkey also had to redefine itself from a multi-ethnic space into a nation state, with one faith and one ethnicity in the absolute majority. Turkey also lived through the experience of treaties, of more or less arbitrary borders, of clashes over borders, of the exchange of populations. Turkey also had to build a new association between state, nation, and territory, as problematic as in other cases.

The Turkish ethnic group was dominant in the ancient Ottoman Empire and the Islamic religion of the Turks was the dominant religion of the Ottoman Empire. But this did not make the task any easier: if anything, it made it more difficult. As we have seen, the Christian communities of the empire were organized according to the *millet* system, on a religious and not ethno-linguistic basis. This was true also and above all for the image Turks had of themselves. The religious category of "believers" was the only important one, and brought Turks together with many ethnic groups (Tartars in Crimea, Circassians, Kara-Kalpaks, Nogai, Albanians, Bosnians, and even Arabs in the Middle East).

In Anatolia, the Turkish ethnic group had spread and become the majority during the centuries when the Ottoman Empire blossomed. But even in 1914, its preeminence was not absolute. In some cities (Constantinople, Smyrna) and in some regions (the Aegean coast), the Turkish population or, more in general, the Islamic ethnicities, were even minorities. On the other hand, the Turkish ethnic group and ethnic groups closely affiliated with the Turks were present not only in the Balkans, but also in the Caucasus, in Iran, in Afghanistan, in Central Asia. Anatolia was not the area of origin of the Turks. On the contrary, the Turkish settlement of Anatolia is recent: it dates back to less than a thousand years. The millennium of geographic distance and sociopolitical divergence has certainly broken the original linguistic unity of many Turkish peoples, and has separated Turks, tartars of the Volga, Bashkirs, Kazaks, Uzbeks, Kirghs.... Nevertheless, in some cases (the Azeris in Azerbaijan, the Turkmen in Turkmenistan) the linguistic differences with the Turks from Anatolia are less pronounced and the separation date is later. With these peoples, it is not unusual to find the definition of ethnic identity operating at two levels, in terms of a local ethn group and a large Turkish people.

In 1918, the ethno-historical complexity of the defeated Ottoman Empire went through the risk of complete fragmentation. In the first place, an intricate game of divisions and differences between Great Britain, France, and Arab allies lead to the separation of all the provinces in the Middle East from the ancient empire. In second place, the treaty of Sèvres, at the same time as the settlements of Versailles and Trianon, attempted to push this logic also onto the soil of Anatolia. To the west, the territories which were to belong to Greece were cut off. To the east, the outline of great Armenia was drawn, but at the same time the Armenians themselves had already been largely eliminated from the region, deported, expelled, or massacred. But above all, the entire southern half of Anatolia was to be divided in two spheres of influence: Italian for the West side (from the Aegean to Konya) and French for the East side (along the entire border with Syria and with the Arab population). The institutional forms of this hegemony were nevertheless not defined.

The national reaction, under the leadership of Mustapha Kemal (Atatürk) was vigorous. A short but violent war with Greece turned the power relations upside down. In 1923, the Sultanate was abolished. A republic was born; Greeks and Armenians remained unsatisfied; the spheres of influence disappeared; the new Turkish state even found favorable settlements on its borders with Syria, Iraq, and the new Soviet Union. Kars and Ardahan, Russian since 1878, were reannexed.

Compared to 1920, the case of today's Turkey is very similar to what we have said about many Central Eastern European countries. Its ethnic and religious makeup has been normalized and homogenized. In the case of Turkey, the ambivalence already present in all the Balkan countries is perhaps even more pronounced. On the one hand, the process seems fully successful, particularly if we consider the initial difficulties: Turkey is a state in full demographic expansion and experiences a particular dynamism in its international relations. On the other hand, the breaks with the past have been particularly hard, a multi-ethnic space which, as we have seen, had been in existence since antiquity. As in all of Eastern Central Europe, there are the peaceful accomplishments and the black holes of violence and ethnic cleansing: the massacre of Armenians during the First World War, the expulsion of the Greeks in the following years, the repression of the Kurds today....

From 1918 to the present, on Turkish soil there have been enacted all the ambivalent strategies we have seen operating for the last century, in the construction of the nation states of the Balkans and Central Eastern Europe: rediscovery and reinvention of a tradition; expulsions and exchanges of population; ethnic fusions; covering up of problems, with the risk of ruinous explosions.

The construction of a new tradition and a new national imaginary, by Kemal Atatürk, brought radical breaks. A state based on religion became secular and sought new ethnic and territorial roots. It is interesting that the roots of the Turkish ethnicity were cut off from those of the Turkish state: there is a pre-Turkish Anatolia, just as there were pre-Anatolian Turks. This has lead to imaginative inventions, designed to emphasize the geographic space of the Turkish people (with slogans like: "from the Atlantic to the Pacific, from Ethiopia to the Arctic Sea"), and the construction of impossible genealogies which included among the ancestors of the Turks peoples of prestige in ancient Asia Minor (for example, the Indo-European Hittites). More constructively, Turkish foreign policy today is constructed under the sign of a double universalism. It considers central to its interests both the people connected by ethno-linguistic links, whatever area they may be in (European Russia; Tartars and Bashkirs; Central Asia; Kirghiz and Kazakhs; Sinkiang Chinese; Uigurs, etc.), and the peoples that were, in the past, involved in the Ottoman territorial expansion (from Albania to Ukraine, from Rumania to Georgia).

In 1923, the great exchange of population between Greeks and Turks ended the many centuries of peaceful coexistence between Christians and Muslims on Anatolian soil. The approximately 170,000 Christians, of various faiths, which today have remained on Turkish soil are but a small part of what was a flourishing population in 1914. In Europe and the Mediterranean in our century, it was often the logic of nation-states, which raised new walls between cultures, civilizations, and religions.

In the space of less than fifty years, a rapid succession of political crises and wars (1878; 1912–13;1914–18; 1920–22) distanced from European soil—and attracted to Anatolian soil—not just Turks, but Moslem people, with the most widely differing roots. After the Second World War, while the migratory flux went in the opposite direction from Europe towards the whole of Europe, new and unpredictable crises attracted other small groups of Turkish peoples to the new Anatolian homeland: in 1951, the Kazaks of Chinese Turkestan wanted to escape the Maoist revolution; in 1979, the Kirghiz of Palmir sought refuge from the Afghan civil war. Turkey in our century has been a land of *muhacir* (immigrants), who received full hospitality from the government, even if not an orderly plan for population. In small and large groups, they settled in the most disparate regions of the country, often in regions abandoned by Greeks, Armenians, or other Christian peoples. With time, the various particular identities have weakened. But the architectural variety of villages in the Anatolian peninsula preserves the memory of the way disparate peoples fused in a new nation.

From the twenties to the present, a threat hangs over the unity of the new Turkish nation-state: the Kurdish question. This question strikes us for two reasons: first of all, the singularity of the destiny of today's Kurds (a form of counter-tendency, one could say), compared to the destiny of other peoples in the region; and, in second place, the numbers involved.

For about a century, the breakup of the Ottoman Empire in the Balkans has given independence to relatively small peoples and national entities, like the Albanians and Macedonians. In the Middle East, various Arab national identities are constituted, united, and divided by thin historical and religious threads. Even the Armenians, the great losers of 1920, found the safety of a new state, no matter how small and precarious, in the Caucasus, which had previously been in the domain of the Czar and the Soviets. By comparison, the Kurds (a people of Iranic language, which nevertheless is quite distinct from the bordering Persians) are more than 22 million, divided in five states: Turkey, Iran, Iraq, Syria, and Armenia. Today, between Turkey and Iraq there is a hot border, which was already a war-line in 1991. Between Turkey and Iran there is an equally hot border: It separates two radically opposite ways of viewing very similar religious roots. But the mental space which unites governments in denying autonomy—and at times even existence—to the Kurds is tragically united.

The recrudescence of the Kurdish conflict on Turkish soil strikes us not because of its foreignness, but, on the contrary, by its familiarity. As in analogous cases in Eastern Central Europe, like the Greeks in Communist Albania, the Turks in Communist Bulgaria, the Kurds are also underestimated in the official census. As happens with the conflicts between Serbs and Albanians, Rumanians and Hungarians, history is there to be minimized, denied, turned upside down. For some official versions, Kurds are only Iranized Turks, when, in fact, the Iranian population in the area is extremely ancient (much more ancient than the Turkish), and the Kurdish ethnicity's roots may go back to pre-Indo-European peoples of the region. On the other hand, the national claims of the Kurds are often unilateral and excessive: all areas of mixed populations are annexed on paper to their state. And the reciprocal violence is fueled in a perverse game, in which, in the end, nobody is right and everybody loses.

The explosion of the multi-national empires has thrown its debris far and wide, both in space and in time.

It has scattered its debris particularly in the Caucasus, for thousands of years a land of conquest and borders between empires: Romans, Parthians, Byzantines, Sassanids, Arabs, Mongols, Persians.... In the centuries of the modern age, the Caucasus became a borderland between the Turkish Ottoman Empire and the Russian Empire. In the last century, it saw the gradual victory of the Russian Empire, carried on by its Soviet successor immediately after World War One. After 1859, the whole of the Caucasus was in Russian hands: both the northern part, and the mountainous southern part, which, along with the internal valleys, is the hardest to control. After 1921, the new Soviet power reestablished its power over the same scenario. After 1991, on the contrary, the Caucasus has broken up into two distinct parts. The northern part stayed in the hands of the principal heir of the Soviet empire: the Russian Federation. The southern part is divided in three states which aspire to being nations, but are full of minorities and areas of mixed populations. Other actors, both internal and external, complicate matters, and conflicts proliferate.

The region's ethnic situation is in many ways different from the traditional European one. On the one hand, the Caucasus has been overrun by the migrations of many peoples originating in Siberia or Central Asia, just like the valley of the Volga of the southern Russian steppes. On the other hand, the population movements have also followed different paths. To the south, in fact, the Caucasus borders the Anatolian peninsula, with the Middle East, and with the Iranian highlands. And from all these areas have come contributions which have created a variegated ethnic panorama in the region. From the Middle East, in particular, has arrived the influence of Islam, already intense in the century following its spread from Mesopotamia and Persia.

In the Caucasus, therefore, we find many Turkic peoples, both on the western and on the eastern side. The most important of these peoples are the Azeris, who are the closest to the Anatolian Turks. They are the descendants of tribes who in the Middle Ages undertook a migration from the Iranian highlands towards the West. We can find some Iranic peoples, belonging to an Indo-European branch which is very important for the Asian population, both in the past and in the present. The most important of these are the Ossetians, closely related to the Scythians and the Alans, who until the first centuries of the Christian era dominated the steppes around the Black Sea. We can find Armenians, an Indo-European people from an autonomous branch, which probably settled in the region at the beginning of the first millennium BC., arriving from the Anatolian peninsula. We can further find many ethnic groups that belong to two linguistic families that are completely different from the ones of bordering peoples. These two families are completely different from each other: nevertheless, until recently it has been common usage to call both Caucasian. At least for the last few millennia (in other words the period we can cover with archaeological and linguistic re-constructions), it seems that the ancestors of these peoples had always been settled there. Nevertheless, in the past, the Caucasian families had a broader distribution: they extended for a good part of the Anatolian peninsula, reaching all the way to Mesopotamia.

The southern Caucasian family (more properly known as Kartvelic) today includes only one people of notable consistency: the Georgians. The western Caucasian family, on the other hand, is very fragmented: Its peoples have often lived (and still do) in isolated valleys with little or no communication. Among the main ones we note the Abkhazians, Chechens, Ingush, Circassians, Kabardinians....

The Caucasus is also crossed by religious borders, which do not always coincide with linguistic borders. The Turkic peoples and many Caucasian peoples are Moslems. But the Azeris are Shiite Moslems (like the majority of the population in bordering Iran, in whose events they often participated). The Armenians are Monophysite Christians, with their own church, autonomous since the High Middle Ages. The Georgians are generally

Orthodox Christians, with considerable Moslem minorities. Some of these minorities sought refuge in the Ottoman Empire during the time of the Russian expansion; others (the Meskets) were deported by Stalin to Central Asia; others still stayed behind and live in the autonomous republic of Agiara, in the southwestern corner of the country, bordering Turkey.

In 1991, the breakup of the Soviet Union produced two types of borders between sovereign states in the Caucasus. One frontier runs from West to East, from the Black Sea to the Caspian Sea, following the mountains, and separating the Russian federation from Georgia, Armenia, and Azerbaijan. Other, much more irregular borders are traced in the valleys of the south side of the Caucasus, and separate the three new states. The new borders are not always drawn along ethno-linguistic borders. Consequently, the transformation of the Soviet Union's internal frontiers to external borders has separated communities that were united for centuries. The diffidence of the Southern states for the large Russian neighbor, and the possibility of the latter's resurgent expansionism, further fuel the fire.

Georgians, Armenians, and Azeris are all peoples with a clearly defined identity, which goes back many centuries, and with religious, linguistic, and historical roots (often the memories of ancient independent kingdoms) which interweave and mutually reinforce each other. Nevertheless, in the last centuries, the southern Caucasus has been the domain of large multi-national empires (Ottoman, Persian, Russian, according to the times and religions), which have variously moved and mixed the three prevailing ethnic groups. This explains not only the many bands of interference and ethnic superimposition which cross the actual borders, but also and above all the fact that the big cities have always had mixed populations, and that in a territory populated by a particular ethnicity there can be inserted vast regions populated by different ethnic groups.

This is particularly the case in the relation between Armenians and Azeris, whose inextricable mixture exploded into a conflict comparable to the Baltic one. In 1989, 391,000 Armenians lived in Azerbaijan (around 5.5% of the entire population of the Republic). They were concentrated in two areas in particular: in Baku, the capital, and in the region of Karabakh. Since then, ethnic cleansing has hit both ways. The Armenian majority in Karabakh proclaimed secession form Azerbaijan, and tried to reconquer an isthmus, a strip of land, with which to reconnect with Armenia, triggering a conflict which still carries on. On the other hand, the Armenian communities of Baku and other cities in the region have been hit by frequent lootings and massacres, and have had to move out and seek refuge in the territories of their new nation state.

Partially different are the processes of fragmentation which today threaten the very existence of Georgia (which in the southern Caucasus occupies the western regions, along, and close to, the coast of the Black Sea). In its border areas, there are minorities of various types: they do not have a state of their own, and nevertheless their identity pushes them somehow to look beyond the new borders. In southwest Agiaria, as we have said, there are Georgian-speaking peoples of Islamic faith: the tendency is to refer to Turkey as a new protector. In the northwestern region, on the border with the Russian federation, live the Abkhazians, Moslems who are a branch of Western Caucasians. Further east, still on the border with the Russian federation, live the Ossetians, of origin, partly Orthodox in faith and partly Moslem.

When, towards the end of 1991, the administrative frontier between the Russian federation and Georgia became an international border, with all the symbolic weight this still carries, both the Abkhazians and the Ossetians felt isolated from the ethnic communities to which they belonged. In the western part of the Caucasus, which today is Russian territory, there lives a sizable fraction of the Ossetian people, along with peoples closely related to the Abkhazians: Adygei, Circassians, Kabardinians. Georgia did not help the situation when it tried to abolish the relative autonomy the ethnic minorities enjoyed during Soviet rule. This was the trigger which made the Abkhazians and Ossetians of Georgia seek secession, a redrawing of borders and their reattachment to the Russian federation. Rather than follow the difficult destiny of a minority in a small state which risks conceiving of itself as mono-national, they prefer to trust in the multi-national aspects of the enormous Russian state.

Today's dramas in the Caucasus closely follow the dramas in many European regions throughout the century: Macedonia, Transylvania, the eastern part of Poland. At present, any border reform could prove unjust for other reasons and in other ways. Those who are favored by the present order would lose out in a different order, and vice versa. As in all cases of new nation states, in the very moment they are formed minorities feel oppressed by the domination of a new majority. As in all cases of nation-states in the formative process, at first glance an unattractive dilemma presents itself: conflict, or population exchanges? Few are the voices that refuse this dilemma, outlining a real alternative: open borders and regional association.

# 15

## Post-Soviet Russia

### The formation of a multi-national state?

On the 25th of December 1991, the lowering of the Soviet flag over the Kremlin marked an historical moment for the two empires which had successively dominated the great Eurasian spaces between the Baltic and the Pacific Ocean. Both empires revolved around Russian ethnicity. They had involved in their expansion innumerable peoples of disparate languages and religions, and had attempted to extend their hegemony in Europe, Asia, and the Middle East.

It was not simply the end of the Soviet Union. Simultaneously, the results of a history started many centuries earlier, under the czars, were canceled. This history started in the latter half of the seventeenth century when Russia, having conquered many of the small peoples and immense spaces of western Asia, expanded westward and southward, at the expense of Poland and the Ottoman Turks (both of which were declining).

The fourteen republics which, during the Soviet years, surrounded the Russian territory like a crown, had already been subjugated under the Czars.

Ukraine ("border"), for centuries a borderland between powerful surrounding authorities (first between Lithuanian and the Mongol-Turkish Khan, then between Poland and the Ottoman Empire), was reached by the Russians in stages, in a slow process which, starting at the end of the sixteenth century from its extreme north-eastern areas, expanded the Czarist empire, in the eighteenth century, to the coast of the Black Sea and the Crimean peninsula.

Estonia was torn from Sweden in the first years of the eighteenth century, around the time when Czar Peter the Great was building, in the far west of his territory, in an area of the Baltic coast at that time populated only by a few Finnish tribes, the new capital which was to bear his name.

At the end of the same century, the agony of the Russian state allowed the Russians to obtain many new lands: the core of today's Latvia, Lithuania, Byelorussia, and other regions of western Ukraine.

In 1801, Russia went over the Caucasian mountains, annexing the ancient Christian kingdom of Georgia. In 1806, it pushed out to the eastern coast of the Caspian sea, populated by Turkish Azerbaijanis. In 1812, it took from the Ottomans Rumanian Bessarabia (Moldavia). In 1828, it conquered the area of Yerevan, populated mostly by Armenians. Only a few decades later was the submission of bellicose mountain peoples completed with the surrender of the Circassians and the Chechens.

As for Central Asia, the long advance southward (started in the second half of the eighteenth century with the progressive vassalization of hordes of nomadic Kazakhs) was completed a century later when, from 1864 to 1895 the Czar's sovereignty included mountains populated by Kirghiz, the oases between Syr Darya and Amu Darya (Tashkent, Samarkand, and Bukhara), extremely ancient Turko-Iranic civilizations, hordes of nomadic Turkmen, and finally the remote valley of Pamir. Only the English push from India succeeded in stopping the Russian movement toward the Indian ocean.

For Russia, the nucleus and the heart of both the Czarist and the Soviet Empire, the 25th of December 1991 meant relinquishing control over strategically very important regions. The entire border area with Central Eastern Europe, from the Baltic to Crimea, was now in the hands of independent and sovereign states whose relations immediately became problematic. In particular, Russian access to the Baltic Sea was reduced to a few windows: the region of Leningrad, the region of Kaliningrad (which, among others, is an *enclave* separate from the main body of the Russian federation), and the north-western Caucasus. The Russian march towards Europe and the warm seas was rudely interrupted.

The incredible rapidity of the collapse of the internal empire has become a source of numerous problems for the Russians.

One of the paradoxical traits of the planned and centralized economy of "real" socialism consisted in a rigid division of labor, so that a particular product was produced in only one republic, city or even factory, to be then exported throughout the entire Union. More than 90% of air conditioners were made in Azerbaijan; buses in Engels (on the lower Volga), refrigerators in Kisinev, in Moldavia; fork lifts, used in shipping, in Leningrad (St. Petersburg). Today, this division is extremely laborious. For the new embryonic regional association, the Commonwealth of Independent States, economic cooperation is vital.

The borders of the new states also present considerable problems. The new external frontier of the Russian federation—in particular, the long borders with Ukraine (1,820 km) and Kazakhstan (7,540 km)—originate in ancient administrative outlines, motivated by the most disparate motives and stratified over a period of centuries. Whatever their original reasons, they clash with many present economic and strategic realities. In particular, the important industrial area of western Siberia is divided in two by the Russian-Kazakh frontier. Above all, there is an abundance of military problems. The new Russian borders do not have any defensive lines, and the cost of creating new defenses would be incalculable. From one perspective, the Red Army still holds its defenses to the borders of the former union. But it obviously leaves open many problems in the case of a civil war in a republic belonging to the CIS, as occurred and is occurring in Tajikistan. Or, in the case of open conflict between two republics of the CIS, like the one between Armenia and Azerbaijan. For states that are the heirs of the Soviet Union, military cooperation is as vital and problematic as economic cooperation.

Russia's new external frontiers are, above all, not ethnic borders. Only the western borders, with Estonia and Latvia, had been borders with independent states and then for less than twenty years. All the other border zones had been areas of imperial expansion, in which Russians had settled for centuries, particularly in the seventeenth and eighteenth centuries. The break-up of the Soviet Union has placed outside the new Russian federation (in the fourteen newly independent republics) more than 25 million people of Russian language and culture. According to the census of 1989, there were 11,427,000 in Ukraine, 6,251,000 in Kazakhstan, 1,652,000 in Uzbekistan, 1,346,000 in Byelorussia, 922,000 in Kirghistan, 906,000 in Latvia, 564,000 in Moldavia, 481,000 in Estonia, and other smaller concentrations.

In the Caucasian republics and in some central Asian republics, already in the preceding decades the Russians had started a sort of reverse migration, returning home. After 1991 the exodus continued and naturally accelerated. This solution is certainly not the most attractive for Russians who have always made their home in the regions of eastern Ukraine and western Kazakhstan, or for the Russians who migrated to the Baltic. On the other hand, the condition of the Russians who are staying behind is beginning to present not insubstantial problems. Some governments in the new states are already engaging in discriminatory practices towards those groups who are perceived as remnants of the Russian occupation.

Furthermore, starting in 1992, new borders are beginning to emerge even *within* the Russian federation, which remains, by far, the largest state in the world.

The new Russian Federation has been defined as a "residual state." In the years of the Czarist Empire, the autocratic government did not give particular privileges to particular areas of the empire. The behavior was perpetuated by the Soviet Union, where the rigid central planning largely ignored the administrative borders between the different republics. Consequently, the Russian ethnic nucleus was accustomed to speaking for the entire empire. This is a significant anomaly in the structure of the Communist party, the true power in the decades of Soviet rule. While in the other republics there were territory-based communist parties, there was no Russian Communist Party. The equivalence between a Soviet Communist Party and a Russian Communist Party seemed natural. Nor was there ever a Russian Academy of Science, or a Russian Writers' Union, but only a Soviet Academy of Sciences, and a Union of Soviet Writers.

Starting in 1992, Russia has to conceive of itself as a single state and transform itself into such a state. And it is a multi-national state, with one clearly dominant nationality (according to the census of 1989, Russians make up 81.5% of the population), but with many ethnicities, of divergent origins, religions, and customs. Alongside very small groupings, are substantial ethnicities (in the Russian federation alone, the Volga Tartars, number about 5.5 million), dispersed over vast territories (in western Siberia, the Yakuts populate an area of 3,000,000 square kilometers. Russia has inherited from the dissolved union the majority of ethnically complex areas: the region between the middle point of the Volga and the Ural mountains (also known as *Idel-Ural*, from the Tartar name for the Volga), the western parts of the Caucasus, and a part of the mountains and internal valleys of the Caucasus.

In the decades of Soviet power a complex territorial system was delineated. The more general administrative units, at the first level, were of three types: regions (*oblast'*), territory (*kraj*) and republics. The *oblasts* were the normal administrative subdivision of the areas with a large Russian majority. The *kraj*, sparsely populated and with a Russian majority, were generally border areas with strategic significance: Stavropol in the Western Caucasus, Altai, and Khabarovsk and Primoriye on the Pacific Ocean.

The republics, on the other hand, were areas populated by other than Russian ethnicities, or areas with mixed populations. In reality, the situation was very varied: the presence of a majority ethnic group next to a Russian minority; the presence of one or more minority ethnic group next to a Russian majority; more or less forced coexistence of two ethnicities with different origins and numbers; contemporaneous presence of many ethnic groups, all definitely minorities. Known as "autonomous" from the old Soviet regime, these republics were supposed to create the conditions for the self-government of the various ethnic groups, particularly at the education and cultural levels. The results were ambivalent, because some successes did not prevent a forced Russianizing. And so, along with the old federated republics of the Soviet Union, in the years of *perestroika* the autonomous republics were also hotbeds of nationalism. At times, the declaration of sovereignty of the autonomous republics went at the same pace as the declaration of independence of the federal republics.

Furthermore, there were two types of second-level units based on ethnicity, which in turn belong to first-level regions or territories. They were the surrounding areas or autonomous region, generally reserved for peoples small in number, spread out over vast territories, or ethnicities with other particular conditions (such as the Jewish Autonomous Region, found in the East).

After 1991, the territorial system was retained but with substantial changes. Some republics changed name, to better underline the rediscovery of their ethnic identity (the Bashkir Republic has become Baskortostan). Some autonomous regions and some autonomous districts were promoted to republics (Adygei, Altai, Khakass, Laracayevo-Cirkassian). One republic split into two, a form of ethnic divorce (Chechen-Ingush has become the Chechen Republic and Republic of the Ingush). Sixteen republics have become twenty-one.

This is the scenario established by the treaty of the 31st of March 1992, through which the old autonomous republics have been transformed into federal republics, with—at least on paper—revived and amplified powers. The treaty was conceived to prevent triggering an ethnic break-up of the new state, similar to the one which had overcome the old Union. Two of the republics did not sign the treaty: the Chechen republic and the Republic of the Tartars. Both sought independence, like the constitutive republics of the dissolved union. Since then, the situation has frozen: the Chechen position is as rigid as the Tartars are inclined to compromise.

Nevertheless, the twenty-one ethnically based federal republics cover 4,876,900 Km$^2$ and include 22,909,200 inhabitants: 28.6% of the surface and 15.5% of the population.

There remains an immense territory of 12,198,500 km$^2$ and 124,476,800 inhabitants which, on its own, would be the largest state in the world!. In this enormous space, which extends for eleven time zones from the Baltic Sea to the Bering Straits, the unity of the Russian population is interrupted only by huge, barely inhabited sections of tundra and forests, in which live small communities of Samoyeds, Paleo-Siberians, Tungus, and Eskimos. And it is precisely the political and administrative structure of this territory which is far from finding equilibrium. In other words: the greatest risk of fragmentation threatening the Russian federation is not ethnic, but rather regional and economic. The needs of the local communities (covered up but not absent in decades of compromises between central and local *nomenklatura*) have come out into the open and require a new national consensus.

The events of the last years have been ambivalent.

On the one hand, the instabilities inside the federation have become very clear. Ethnically based localisms on a regional and economic basis have appeared in the entire region populated by Russians: the presence of real internal customs tariffs; difficulties in exporting certain products outside production areas; the use of local coupons instead of state money.... Faced with this crisis and the power struglles which hit Moscow in 1991 and 1993, the local authorities have been tempted to submit their territories to their sovereignty and their decisions, almost eliminating the presence of overriding laws and authorities. From 1991 to 1993, in fact, many territorial entities have maintained the supremacy of their respective constitutions over the constitution of the federation as a whole. Some regions (Vologda, for instance) and some territories (Krasnojarsk) have asked to be considered on a par with ethnically-based federal republics. A secessionist sentiment has even appeared in some of the areas most distant from the nucleus of the Russian state: in Siberia, and above all on the East coast, which hopes to come into the economic orbit of Japan.

On the other hand, the inadequacy of the present balance between center and periphery has opened a debate on possible reforms and transformations. In 1989, when the Russian federation was still the most conspicuous part of the Soviet union, the geographer Vladimir Sokolov proposed a project of territorial reorganization, which remains timely today now that Russia has become a nation-state proper. Drawing on the American federal experience,

Sokolov proposed dividing Russian territory ethnically into around thirty republics with comparable demographic weight, corresponding to large economic regions: European Russia, the Urals, Western Siberia, Eastern Siberia, the region of Lake Baikal, the Far East and so on. In European Russia, for example, the traditional regions would be replaced by eight new republics with increased powers: the region of Moscow, the northern Caucasus, central Russia (Smolensk), Povolye (the lower Volga), eastern Russia (around St. Petersburg), southern Russia (Voronez), the Baltic Republic (Kaliningrad), and Karelia. Along with the Russian territory, there would, naturally, also be space for republics of other ethnicities.

After the breakup of the Soviet Union, this way of rethinking and conceiving the territory has involved not so much theory as the actions of the present administrative units, ethnically based Russian regions and federal republics. In fact, bordering regions and republics have often come together to outline networks of economic cooperation, which act as an embryonic restructuring of the Russian Federation's territory. There exists an Association of the Volga (Russian regions of Astrakhan, Carachai, Nizhni-Novgorod, Penza, Samara, Saratov, Simbirsk, the Kalmuck, Chuvash, Mordvinian, and Tartar Republics), an Association of the Urals (Russian regions of Chelyabinsk, Ekaterinenburg, Kurgan, Orenburg, Perm, Tyumen, Bashkir and Udmur Republics), a Siberian Charter, a Far East Association....

Disintegration and association: which process will prevail?

Starting in 1992, Russia has found itself trapped in a double identity: between the identity of the old empire and the identity of a new multi-national and multi-regional state, which must revise the rules for internal coexistence. Consequently, it has found itself facing a double risk: the risk of further implosion (both regional and ethnic), and the risk of a nostalgic need for revenge, bent on constructing a third empire, searching for new annexations or perhaps only seeking new limited sovereignties.

The middle way between disintegration and expansion is subtle. Will it be achievable?

Starting in 1992, the Russian identity crisis has become a crucial problem for all Europe. At the same time, an equally crucial problem is the identity-crisis of the republics which have broken off from the center in Moscow, and look to Europe for their economic reference point, and to NATO for their military reference point.

# 16

## Conclusion

### The complexity of Europe

At the beginning of the nineties, identity crises and processes of disintegration have involved states and collectivities throughout Europe.

The end of the multi-national states (the Soviet Union, Yugoslavia, Czechoslovakia) is only the most dramatic aspect of these crises, which also are manifested by ethnic conflicts (between Rumanians and Hungarians in Transylvania, Flemish and Walloons in Belgium, Russians and Moldavians, Armenians and Azeris), demands for rebirths and self-government from old nationalities (Basques, Catalans, Scots), requests for greater regional autonomy and federalist reforms (Italy, Ukraine), the emergence of new units of trans-border cooperation (the Euro-regions on the border between Germany and Poland, Tyrol between Austria and Italy), and questions about the future form of that enormous multi-ethnic and still centralized state that is Russia, today exposed to the threat of the worst nationalist excesses....

After 1914–18, the absolute sovereignty of nation-states was seen as the most adequate formula to resolve the instabilities following the end of the great multi-national empires, which for centuries had dominated eastern central Europe.

After 1989–91, the absolute sovereignty of nation-states clearly shows its limits. It has been a source of conflicts every time it has crystallized and emphasized borders. And it is again the absolute sovereignty of nation-states that has made inter-ethnic conflicts so explosive, particularly in areas where peoples and nationalities are mixed.

For about a century or so, throughout Europe, borders between states have been modeled on ethnic borders. The disintegration of the Soviet Union, Czechoslovakia and Yugoslavia seems to have brought the equivalence between state and nation to its completion.

Nevertheless, viewed from closer up, the apparent ethnic homogeneity of the European states hides innumerable diversities.

Almost all the European nation-states are in some form multi-ethnic, with their majorities and their minorities. Furthermore, individuals of one nationality often live outside the borders of their nation-state. A nationality, therefore, tends to view as inherent to its territory all the areas inhabited by individuals who belong to that nationality, inside or outside the borders of their own state. Naturally, the areas located outside the borders of one state belong to the territory of another state. In this way, in numerous cases of ethnic mixes, nations' territories inevitably are superimposed upon each other.

Nationalities are not defined (depending on the case) simply by sharing a language or religion.

Very important for an individual of a given nationality is the feeling of sharing with others a common destiny, the feeling of belonging to an uninterrupted history that connects him or her to common roots in the near and distant past. Every nation has its own myths, its events, its founding heroes. In most cases, these myths, these events, these founding heroes are tied to particular times and spaces. Frequently, these are tied to places which today are outside the state's borders, and which are presently inhabited by individuals with other common destinies, from other nations. Nevertheless, these places continue to be a part of the nation's territory, in another conception of the term, which involves history, culture, roots, and a people's collective imagination.

In our century, the dramatic history of central and eastern Europe has produced and imposed great movements of people. The governments and international powers that wanted or favored these movements aspired to a greater national homogeneity, reducing the number of ethnic minorities, so that every individual would be located within the borders of his or her respective nation-state. In other words, the European map of our time derives from an appalling attempt to reduce, as much as possible, the superimpositions between different nation-states. But these movements of peoples were not (and are not and never will be) complete. The ancient ethnic mixtures have not disappeared. The ancient minorities return, aware of their identities. At times, border changes have created new minorities and ethnic mixes. New minorities and new ethnic mixes continue to emerge, for the most disparate reasons: economic migrations, influxes of refugees, pressure the entire planet on the European continent, and the integration of citizens in the European Community.

Above all, no modification of the borders and the ethnic population of the territories can act coherently and necessarily on a nationality's ties with places, spaces, cities, sanctuaries.... In 1912 as in 1993, an important factor in the hostilities among Balkan nations has been (and is) the fact that three different nations feel a strong link to Macedonia. This region belonged several times to the Byzantine Empire, it was the nucleus of the Bulgarian empire of Simeon (tenth century), and was also part of the Serb Empire of Stefan Dusan (fourteenth century). No exchange of population, no ethnic variation has ever removed the various peoples' profound ties of the to this region.

Often the citizens of a nation emigrate or are forced to leave. But a nation's culture rarely forgets its own roots and its founding myths. At times, the tie with myths and roots becomes even stronger when a territory which belonged to one group in ancient times is inherited by other states, by other nations.

The multi-dimensionality of nations and their territories, the multiple superimpositions, the intertwined coexistence of diversities within the collectivity seeking to develop its own unitary identity, seem to be irreducible traits of European civilization, in the present as in the past.

In our century, the totalitarian freezing of history was accompanied by the illusion that it was possible to intervene on a people's collective imagination, that it was possible to decide by decree on the destiny of a historical memory, that it was possible to extend or contract a nation's territory at will, in all senses of the term. The failure of these illusions is one of the reasons for the present nationalist, ethnic, and localist explosions, which are at times also linked to these same illusions, the same willingness to simplify, to their own exclusive advantage, that which is inevitably superimposed, multidimensional, and complex.

The European ruling powers in our century have taken for granted the possibility of compressing to one plane the multiple meanings and dimensions of a state's territory and history. Today, the complexity of connections between states, nations, ethnicities and individuals threatens to destroy the balance which has been consolidated over time. Many conflicts have to do precisely with the conditions of individuals and collectivities at the crossroads of different territories and different historical representations. The secession of the Serbs in Croatia and Bosnia has shown the barbarity which conditions of this kind create. The disintegration of the Soviet Union has multiplied the dangers: the condition of Russians outside Russia threatens the stability not only of the region's new republics, but all of Europe. To this day, the whole of Eastern Central Europe presents many precarious conflicts.

The present representation of borders and interactions among nations is too limited and too limiting. We need new images and concepts which at times require superimpositions and multiplications of sovereignty. With a new sensibility for multiple and collective identities, we need to look for new opportunities, precisely where the dangers of conflict appear greatest.

At the end of this century, crucial new questions are being asked of Europe: can new political and institutional mechanisms emerge from an understanding of the interconnections and complexities of its histories and memories? Can those forms of integration emerge between the various areas of our continent, which a mechanical transposition of economic criteria and economists has seemed unable to guarantee?

The identity of an individual depends in a decisive and irreversible way on all the relations and all the interactions which he or she entertains or entertained with other individuals and multiple collectivities. Similarly, the features of state, national, and regional identities depend, in a decisive and irreversible way, upon the relations and the interactions which every state, every nation, and every region entertains or has entertained with other states, nations, and regions. Throughout European history there has been a constant defining of relations and interactions (institutional, political, economic, cultural, religious, spiritual) among states, nations, and regions.

These relations and interactions have united, divided, transformed and intertwined. The nations of Europe have always been steeped in diversities, and have found in these diversities a fundamental reason for their vitality. All the nations of Europe are the results of tormented and often improbable syntheses, between heterogeneous roots, originating in many areas and from many actors of the European population. Every place in Europe has a stratified memory of these histories and these contributions.

In five crucial years, from 1989 to 1994, Europe has shown all its faces, with a spectrum of breadth and ambivalence which are literally intolerable, from hope to desperation, from solidarity to barbarism. Only by looking deeply into all these faces will we be able to understand the roots of the future.

On the fateful and fatal day of the fall of the Berlin wall we could only note, with some confusion, that nothing in Europe would be the same again.

For an instant, the horizon of a Europe both united and manifold appeared, no longer dominated by bilateral polarizations and characterized instead by respect, and the proliferation and interaction of local diversities.

Today, the prospect of a European confederation which safeguards both unity and multiplicity has become dramatically less likely. It has become much more improbable. But precisely as it has become more improbable it has also become more necessary. Every day, all serious problems appear literally insoluble at the simple level of nation-states: from the environmental crisis to the conversion of the economy in the states of Eastern Central Europe, to cooperation with the southern hemisphere. In particular, all forms of coexistence on European soil threaten to implode. The only reply to this implosion is the construction of a broadened community, with "broadened" values.

In the space of a few years, what has changed is not so much the extensions and the forms the future coexistence of the European peoples will be able to have. Certainly, projects and strategies of economic, institutional and military integration have been put in place: a Europe at several speeds, a multiplication of institutions, regional associations, Euro-regions, partnerships for peace.... But the main front is another one. It is the disengagement of the rhetoric—victorious in our century, and in which we are still profoundly immersed—that has emphasized the ideas of purification and of the separation of individual and collective diversity. It is the creation of a common European imagination, a common memory, a common tradition, of myths and rites in which to embody the values of encounter, comparison, interaction, and the hybridization of different individual and collective experiences.

An important step towards this end consists in unearthing, valuing, narrating, viewing from many perspectives, listening to, and interweaving all the stories and all the memories, all the times and all the spaces that have generated and continue to generate our province of Europe, this small community of destiny within the great planetary community of destiny.

# References

Agursky, M. (1987) *The Third Rome: National Bolshevism in the USSR.* Westview Press, Boulder.

Anderson, P., Aymard, M., Bairoch, P., Barberis, W., Ginzburg, C. Eds. (1993) *Storia d'Europa. 1. L'Europa oggi.* Einaudi, Torino.

Argentieri, F. Eds (1991) *La fine del blocco sovietico.* Ponte alle Grazie, Firenze.

Ash, T. G. (1992) *Le rovine dell'Impero. Europa centrale 1980–1990.* Italian Translation. Mondadori, Milano.

Balbo, L., Manconi, L. (1990) *I razzismi possibili.* Feltrinelli, Milano.

Balta, P. eds. (1992) *La Méditerranée réinventée. Réalités et espoirs de la coopération.* La Découverte, Paris.

Banac, I. (1984) *The National Question in Yugoslavia. Origins History Politics.* Cornell University Press, Ithaca.

Bartlett, R. (1993) *The Making of Europe. Conquest Colonization and Cultural Change. 950–1350.* Allen Lane, London.

Bibó, I. (1993) *Misère des petits États d'Europe de l'Est.* Albin Michel, Paris.

Bocchi G., Ceruti, M. (1993) *Origini di storie.* Feltrinelli, Milano.

Bocchi, G., Ceruti, M., Morin, E. (1991) *L'Europa nell'era planetaria.* Sperling & Kupfer, Milano.

Boffa, G. (1976) *Storia dell'Unione Sovietica*. Mondadori, Milano.

Bogdan, H. (1991) *Histoire des pays de l'Est. Des origines à nos jours*. Perrin, Paris.

Boockmann, H., Schilling, H., Stürmer, M. (1990) *La Germania. Dall'antichità alla caduta del muro*. Italian Translation. Laterza, Roma-Bari.

Brossat, A., Combe, S., Potel, J.-Y., Szurek, J.-C. eds. (1990) *À l'Est, la mémoire retrouvée*. La Découverte, Paris.

Bulloch, J., Morris, H. (1992) *No Friends but the Mountains. The Tragic History of the Kurds*. Viking Press, London.

Buttino, M. ed. (1993) *In a Collapsing Empire. Underdevelopment, Ethnic Conflicts and Nationalisms in the Soviet Union*. Feltrinelli, Milano.

Caratini, R. (1992) *Dictionnaire des nationalités et des minorités de l'ex-URSS*. Larousse Paris.

Castellan, H. (1991) *Histoire des Balkans*. Fayard, Paris.

Collotti, E. (1968) *Storia delle due Germanie. 1945–1968*. Einaudi, Torino

Collotti, E. (1992) *Dalle due Germanie alla Germania unita*. Einaudi, Torino.

Conte, F. (1995) *The Slavs*. Boulder: East European Monographs.

Dann, O. (1993) *Nation und Nationalismus in Deutschland. 1770–1990*. Beck, München.

Delannoi, G., Morin, E. eds. (1987) *Eléments pour une théorie de la nation*. Communications, 45.

Delors, J. (1992) *Le nouveau concert européen*. Editions O Jacobs, Paris.

Dini, P. U. (1991) *L'anello baltico. Profilo delle nazioni baltiche Lituania Lettonia Lstonia*. Marietti, Genova.

Drakulic, S. (1993) *Balkan Express: Fragments from the Other Side of War*. W. W. Norton & Co., New York.

Duby, G. ed. (1977) Histoire de la France. Larousse, Paris.

Fejtö, F. (1986) *Mémoires. De Budapest à Paris*. Calmann-Lévy, Paris.

Fejtö, F. (1988) *Requiem pour un empire défunt: histoire de la destruction de l'Autriche-Hongrie*. lieu commun, Paris.

Fejtö, F., Kulesza-Mietkowski, E. (1992) *La fin des démocraties pop-ulaires. Les chemins du post-communisme*. Seuil, Paris.

Ferro, M. ed. (1993) *L'État de toutes les Russies. Les États et les nations de l'ex-URSS*. La Découverte, Paris.

Forsyth, J. (1992) A *History of the Peoples of Siberia*. Cambridge University Press, Cambridge.

Fossier, R. ed. (1986) *The Cambridge History of the Middle Ages. The New Worlds. 350-950*. Cambridge University Press, New York.

Fossier, R. ed. (1988) *The Cambridge History of the Middle Ages. The New Worlds. 950-1250*. Cambridge University Press, New York.

Fossier, R. ed. (1987) *Storia del Medioevo. Il tempo delle crisi, 1250–1520*. Italian Translation. Einaudi, Torino.

Foucher, M. (1991) *Fronts et frontières. Un tour du monde géo-politique*. Fayard, Paris.

Foucher, M. ed. (1993) *Fragments d'Europe*. Fayard, Paris.

Furet, F. (1992) *Revolutionary France 1770–1880*. Blackwell, Oxford.

Furet, F. ed. (1989) *L'Héritage de la révolution français*. Hachette, Paris.

Galli, G. (1989) *Hitler e il nazismo magico*. Rizzoli, Milano.

Garde, P. (1992) *Vie et mort de la Yougoslavie*. Fayard, Paris.

Gieysztor, A. (1979) *History of Poland*. Polish Scientific Publishers, Warsaw.

Giordan, H. ed. (1992) *Les minorités en Europe. Droits linguistiques et droits de l'homme*. Kimé, Paris.

Grmek, M., Gijdara, M., Simac, N. eds. (1993) *Le nettoyage ethnique. Documents historiques sur une idéologie serbe*. Fayard, Paris.

Guoimar, J.-Y. (1990) *La Nation entre l'histoire et la raison*. La Découverte, Paris.

Haugen, E., McClure, J. D., Thomson, D. S. (1981) *Minority Languages Today.* Edinburgh University Press, Edinburgh.

Havel, V. (1990) *Interrogatorio a distanza.* Italian Translation. Garzanti, Milano.

Hobsbawm, E. J. (1990) *Nations and Nationalisms Since 1780: Programme, Myth, Reality.* Cambridge University Press, New York.

Krejci, J., Velímsky, V. (1981) *Ethnic and Political Nations in Europe.* Croom Helm, London.

Lacoste, Y. (1993) *Dictionnaire de Géopolitique.* Flammarion, Paris.

Lorot, P. (1991) *Le réueil balte.* Hachette, Paris.

Macartney, C. A. (1971) *The Habsburg empire.* Weidenfeld and Nicolson, London.

Magas, B. (1993) *The Destruction of Yugoslavia. Tracking the Breakup 1980–92.* Verso, London.

Mammarella, G. (1988) *Storia d'Europa dal 1945 a oggi.* Laterza, Roma-Bari.

Mantran, R. ed. (1989) *Histoire de l'Empire Ottoman.* Fayard, Paris.

Martiniere, G., Varela, C. eds. (1992) *L'État du Monde en 1492.* La Découverte, Paris.

Matvejevic, P. (1991) *Mediterraneo. Un nuovo breviario.* Italian Translation. Garzanti, Milano.

Michnik, A. (1993) *La seconda rivoluzione. L'Europa dell'Est e la costruzione della democrazia.* Italian Translation. Sperling & Kupfer, Milano.

Milosz, Cz. (1985) *La mia Europa.* Italian Translation. Adelphi, Milano.

Milosz, Cz. (1990) *De la Baltique au Pacifique.* Fayard, Paris.

Minczeles, H. (1993) *Vilna, Wilno, Vilnius. La Jérusalem de Lituanie.* La Découverte, Paris.

Mink, G., Szurek, J.-C. eds. (1992) *Cet étrange post-communisme. Rupture et transitions en Europe centrale et orientale.* La Découverte, Paris.

Missiroli, A. (1991) *La questione tedesca. Le due Germanie dalla divisione all'unità. 1945–1990.* Ponte alle Grazie, Firenze.

Mommsen, M. ed. (1992) *Nationalismus in Ost Europa.* Beck, München.

Morin, E. (1988) *Pensare l'Europa.* Italian Translation. Feltrinelli, Milano.

Morin, E. (1989) *Per uscire dal ventesimo secolo.* Italian Translation. Lubrina, Bergamo.

Morin, E. (1989) *Vidal et les siens.* Seuil, Paris.

Morin, E., Kern, A. B. (1994) *Terra-Patria.* Italian Translation. Cortina, Milano.

Nahaylo, B., Swoboda, V. (1991) *Soviet Disunion. A history of the Nationalities Problem in the USSR.* Free Press, New York.

Nahoum-Grappe, V. ed. (1993) *Vukouar, Sarajevo.* Esprit, Paris.

Nolte, E. (1988) *La guerra civile europea. 1917–1945.* Italian Translation. Sansoni, Firenze.

Pearson, R. (1983) *National Minorities in Eastern Europe.* Macmillan, London.

Philippart, E. ed. (1993) *Nations et frontières dans la nouvelle Europe.* Complexe, Bruxelles.

Pirjevec, J. (1993) *Il giorno di San Vito. Jugoslavia 1918–1992. Storia di una tragedia.* Italian Translation. Nuova Eri, Torino.

Planhol, X. De (1993) *Les nations du prophète. Manuel géographique de politique musulmane.* Fayard, Paris.

Pomian, K. (1990) *L'Europa e le sue nazioni.* Italian Translation. Il Saggiatore, Milano.

Puech, H.-C. ed. (1977) *Storia delle religioni. Il Cristianesimo da Costantino a Giovanni XXIII.* Italian Translation. Laterza, Roma-Bari.

Riasanovsky, N. V. (1984) *A History of Russia.* 4th ed. Oxford University Press, New York.

Rizzo, A. (1993) *Big Bang. Il cambiamento italiano nel cambiamento mondiale.* Laterza, Roma-Bari.

Romano, S. (1991) *Disegno della storia d'Europa dal 1789 al 1989. Trionfo, morte e resurrezione degli Stati nazionali.* Longanesi, Milano.

Roux, M. ed. (1992) *Nations État et Territoire en Europe de l'est et en URSS.* L'Harmattan, Paris.

Rusconi, G. E. (1987) *Rischio 1914. Come si decide una guerra.* Il Mulino, Bologna.

Rusconi, G. E. (1990) *Capire la Germania. Un diario ragionato sulla questione tedesca.* Il Mulino, Bologna.

Rusconi, G. E. (1993) *Se cessiamo di essere una nazione. Tra etno-democrazie regionali e cittadinanza europea.* Il Mulino, Bologna.

Rywkin, M. (1988) *Russian Colonial Expansion to 1917.* Mansell, London.

Salvi, S. (1990) *La disUnione Sovietica.* Ponte alle Grazie, Firenze.

Sanguin, A. -L. ed. (1993) *Les minorités ethniques en Europe.* L'Harmattan, Paris.

Sellier, A., Sellier, J. (1991) *Atlas des peuples d'Europe Centrale.* La Découverte, Paris.

Sellier, J., Sellier, A. (1993) *Atlas des peuples d'Orient.* La Découverte, Paris.

Shirer, W. L. (1960) *The Rise and Fall of the Third Reich; A History of Nazi Germany.* Simon and Schuster, New York.

Shirer, W. L. (1986) *Gli anni dell'incubo. 1930–1940.* Italian Translation. Mondadori, Milano.

Sked, A. (1989) *Decline and Fall of the Habsburg Empire. 1815–1918.* Longman, London.

Smith, A. D. (1992) *The Ethnic Origins of Nations.* Basil Blackwell, London.

Tilly, C. (1991) *Coercion, Capital, and European States. A.D. 990–1990.* Cambridge, Mass: Basil Blackwell.

Tilly, C. (1993) *European Revolutions. 1492–1992.* Blacwell, Cambridge, Mass.

Veinstein, G. ed. (1992) *Salonique 1850–1918. La "ville des Juifs" et le réveil des Balkans.* Autrement, Paris.

Yerasimos, S. (1993) *Questions d'Orient. Frontières et minorités des Balkans au Caucase.* La Découverte, Paris.

# Conflict and Consciousness
## Studies in War, Peace, and Social Thought

This is a new series of texts designed to address the unprecedented threat to humanity posed by conventional warfare and nuclear weapons. The principal aim of this series is to illuminate the often opaque connections that link individual consciousness, personal and collective belief systems, and social practices involving coercion and violence. Since the reasons for wars and the prospects for an enduring peace transcend conventional academic disciplinary boundaries, this series will include cross-disciplinary and unorthodox approaches, as well as more traditional philosophical, social-scientific, and humanistic monographs.

The series editor is:

Charles P. Webel

Department of Philosophy
California State University
Chico, CA 95929-0730

Department of Anthropology
University of California
Berkeley, CA 94720